LEAD WITH
V.I.V.A.

LEAD WITH
V.I.V.A.

*Stories and Strategies of Leaders
Who Lead with Vision, Inspiration,
Voice, and Acceptance*

LEAD WITH V.I.V.A.

Stories and Strategies of Leaders Who Lead with Vision,
Inspiration, Voice, and Acceptance

Copyright © 2019 by Lead with V.I.V.A.

All Rights Reserved

Paperback ISBN: 978-0-9996121-5-6

Published by TopLeadershipExperts.com

Editor: Shareen Rivera
Photo Credits: Julian Carmona with Capture-Pro L.A.

CONTENTS

INTRODUCTION

Congratulations on setting aside quality time only for yourself, and by beginning to dive into this life-transforming book that shares all the authentic stories where the authors used their voice to prevail through all the hardships they have been through. You are the person we had in mind as we made progress in publishing this book. It makes me happy to know that I am the channel through which they are able to share with you this book, as a publisher, I always look for authentic stories that not only can inspire and empower but also equips the readers for success in their personal and professional life.

In the time that you are investing in reading this book, you will find the awakening moments where each author shared their inspiration and how that helped them overcome challenges and thrive to the point where they are now. The voice and inspiration they use will help guide you to the level of achievement and happiness that you are looking for. They shared stories and practical strategies for you to get to know them and to implement them in your own life.

It has been said that having a vision is being able to see beyond what you can see, throughout this book, you will be able to see how the authors used the power of vision to feel the way they desired and to acquire the things they desire and to build the experiences they wished for. One of the most transformational decisions we can make in our lives regardless of where we are, is the decision to accept ourselves the way we are and to recognize the power within us to make the necessary changes to use voice inspiration vision and acceptance as our main vehicle for us to have a happy and fulfilled life full of passion and purpose.

You are about to embark on a journey that will show you many different paths for you to use your own personal power through voice inspiration vision and acceptance to where you can feel and accomplish everything in your life that you most desire.

Connect with me and each author through different social media channels for you to continue this journey of happiness and fulfillment through the stories and strategies you have learned in this book. We want to learn from your story as well. Now, go on, my friend. We are happy you found, "Lead with V.I.VA."

To your success,

Ovi Vasquez
#LeadWithVIVA

MIA PEREZ

The Birth Of V.I.V.A.

I stood on the stage absorbing the moment. A crowd of women standing on their feet in applause. Hugging, crying of excitement and bonding with one another. It was the end of the night for our 4th V.I.V.A. Women's Empowerment Community GALA in just a little over one year of having started V.I.V.A. I was in awe of how just the prior year, on a scorching hot summer day of July 2017, a small group of about 25 women gathered for the 1st event which I hosted in my backyard. Just three days prior to that event only ten women had reserved to come, TOTAL! The ten included the four speakers, the moderator, decorator, my mother, my roommate, and two friends. Basically, only the ones involved.

I was very discouraged and was even advised to cancel the entire thing. As persistent as I am though, I flooded those inboxes, texts and phone calls, "Hey Girl, soooo you ARE coming RIGHT?" Twenty-five women attended that day, and VIVA began. Fast forward to October 2018, here we were! Over 100 women all dressed in their beautiful black dresses, with their masquerades in the theme of "The Mask We Hide Behind". As the Founder of V.I.V.A., this was truly an emotional day! I stood on that stage gazing at the hundred faces of women clapping for V.I.V.A. with hope in their eyes while my own eyes scanned the room. It was as if it played in slow motion before me while my memory took me back to the very day when I had envisioned this moment.

It was a late afternoon in the Fall of 2011. A day I will never forget. I had just left my house in the middle of an anxiety attack, sweating and short of breath. My body went from hot to cold and then back to hot. I wanted to scream but I couldn't. I felt like my heart was going to beat out of my chest! As I drove up a nearby hill, my body now felt safe enough to release all that tension and I began to cry. I was forced to pull over at almost the very top because I had begun to weep so much, to the point that I could no longer see. I believe everything happens for a reason and God had a reason for me there that day. You see, as I sat parked on that hill, wiping my tears, I witnessed one of the most spectacular sunsets before me. It was so incredible it would have taken your breath away! I just sat there and watched, completely mesmerized by its beauty as if all else had disappeared. However, as captivated as I was by that glorious sunset, something else happened. I noticed that as I watched the sun slowly begin to vanish before me into the horizon, a new sadness overcame me for I could feel myself slowly fading with it. The tears began to flow yet again, because for the first time in many years it actually hit me; I realized how much I missed my own light.

What happened to me? Where did that girl go? That girl that I used to be so full of life. That light was no longer there! Now as the night took over, sadly enough, I identified more with the darkness, because the darkness translated into emptiness and sadly, that was a much more familiar feeling to me feeling empty. To be honest, if it wasn't for the fact that I had a 4-year old daughter I'd be leaving behind, I might have just ended my life that very day as many people do when they feel they have nothing left to live for. After all, my life had already been taken from me anyway and I was dead inside BUT God had another plan for me. This is where the first letter of V.I.V.A. was born.

Exactly 7 years back from this GALA, on that hill. And even though my hopes and dreams had been stripped from me, with tears running down my cheeks, I mustered up the courage to decide to change my situation and find the light again. I looked at myself in the rearview mirror and said out loud, "I AM WORTH IT!". I don't know if I really believed it for myself in that moment, but growing up in church, I recalled that "faith first comes by hearing". Sometimes even if you don't believe it just yet, the best thing you can do is *speak things out loud over your life and into existence.*

What I did believe, undoubtedly, was that my 4-year-old daughter deserved for me to give myself another chance for me and her, but especially FOR HER. I promised God that day, that if he allowed me to get out of the mess I was in and start fresh one day, that I would create a space for women where we would gather together. A space where I would breathe hope and inspiration into them and into one another. So, it was that day, on that hill in late 2011, that I dared myself to Dream Again. V.I.V.A – It all starts with a **VISION**!

Before I move forward, I must warn you that I am going to be very real and explicit within the next page and a half. If you are a victim or survivor, this may trigger you so you may want to skip to the next page. This is my truth though and it's part of my story.

Today, I am a proud full-time single mother of a 12-year-old daughter. She is my reason and she is my everything. I thank God for her every day.

I was married in 2006. The marriage was over before she turned 4 years old, but he did not leave the house for another three years. During that period, I was forced to "play house" and pretend

3

things were ok. But no one would have ever imagined the hell I lived in for all those years. To be honest, I didn't know myself how bad it was at the time. How did I NOT know? Let me explain. When you are in an abusive relationship, it doesn't happen suddenly; however, one day it just hits you. You wake up and sadly, you no longer recognize the person staring back at you in the mirror. By then you are so far gone and sucked into their web that you are paralyzed in fear. Not only have you lost your way, but you have lost hope. It is much like the parable of the boiled frog. They say that if you place a frog in boiling water, the frog will leap right out. On the other hand, if you place the frog in a pot of tepid water and slowly bring it to a boil, the frog will never jump out because the subtle increase of the temperature will slowly acclimate it. The poor frog will remain there without noticing and boil to death in that water.

That is what it is like to be with an abuser. They slowly and gradually take away your identity, every piece of who you are. They pick you apart daily, stripping you down layer-by-layer, and you do not even see it coming. They cut you, and then they stitch you, they wound you and then nurse you. They destroy you and break you down with words, and then they apologize because if they did not "LOVE" you so much, they would not become so angry and behave that way. Every day you walk on eggshells to make sure you do not say the wrong thing, or you are in a daze still recovering from the last arguments of what "you" caused and you are living in a constant state of apology. You cannot even address anything or begin to sort through things in your head because you are in a foggy state of confusion. Now you've arrived where they want you and this is how they intend to keep you. Abusers take over your life, little-by-little until you have no opinion, no voice. You are made to feel, and eventually, you believe that you are irrelevant. Your sole purpose is now to serve them. They will feed you the scraps of their love and torture you mentally, emotionally handicapping you until you are at their mercy. You are too scared to leave, and you convince yourself that it is better to stay, so you do. They target us, the givers.

You are worthy of love and so much more. My prayer for you is that through this book you will find your voice if you have lost yours and along with it, a journey of healing. I survived pretty much every form of abuse in the abuse spectrum. Sometimes you don't know how bad things are until you remove yourself from the people or situation, because in the midst of it, you are so caught up in just "surviving" that all you can manage to do is remember to inhale, exhale. That was me, I was just trying to survive every day. Brain fogged, walking on eggshells, constant verbal and emotional beating down, made to question my own sanity, financially cut off from all access to money and raped by my own husband in order to pay my cell phone bill, gas or groceries to feed OUR daughter. Yes, you read it correctly, RAPE. You may think, "Mia, that's a pretty serious accusation". Well, it was NOT consensual sex and I didn't even know the reality of what it was until I shared this in a therapy session after I left.

Even though we were no longer together, we lived in the same house, and he would remind me that the fact that I bore his last name made me HIS and until I didn't carry his name any longer, I had an obligation to him. So, it wouldn't matter if I said no, if I cried and pleaded, and it didn't matter if my daughter laid asleep next to me. He would force himself on me until I would have to go into the spare bedroom in fear he would wake my daughter, so he could have his way. The spare bedroom was dark, like the moments themselves that I laid there like a corpse. The alcoholic breath repulsed me and made my skin crawl. The first few times were unbearable, painful and humiliating. Especially the times he had abused a stronger "substance" because that meant it would happen for hours to the point that I would bleed. Eventually, I would learn to not fight back and just lay there because his 220-pound body would overpower my struggle anyway.

Your subconscious mind has extraordinary power in controlling your life experiences. For example, in the midst of that type of trauma, your body trains your mind after a while to check out mentally and emotionally so that it numbs itself. It's a type of defense mechanism. That's exactly what I would do because it was my only safe place in order to survive those moments. I often wondered if hell was any worse while I would endure that and I'm sure it's pretty close to it. I don't wish that on anyone. Here I was, a prostitute in my own home in order to purchase food, pay for my phone bill and provide the bare necessities for my daughter and I. Except, my pimp was my own husband. This was my life prior to V.I.V.A. This was the root of my tears, the feeling of darkness and emptiness that day. Because as beautiful as the sunset was and as dark as it had become, as I sat in my car, I looked down and I could still see the bloodstains on my pants after leaving that dreadful spare bedroom. This time though, I had made a decision that would change my life forever. Sometimes we remain stuck in terrible situations waiting for a fully thought out and fail-proof game plan in order to make a move when in reality, you just need to move!

> *"Visionaries look into the future and see things not through the lens of current reality, but through the lens of future possibility." Kara Claypool*

We all have encountered disappointments at some point in our lives. We've all had our dreams crushed, people walk out on us, abandon us, failed careers, failed relationships and at times it's us that have let ourselves down because we put others above us, sacrificing our own dreams. In the end, they walk away fulfilled after we've given our all and they have emptied us of ourselves. If we all have experienced setbacks though, what sets a Leader apart? It's the one who dares to Dream Again! Those that choose to set their eyes on something greater that lies ahead instead of drowning in their current reality. They don't even have to know what that will be, they simply choose to trust in a future possibility.

Always remember this, despite your situation, you have the power to determine your future outcome. Had I focused on my current reality, I wouldn't be where I am today, and V.I.V.A. wouldn't exist.

Ironically, my worst nightmare offered me the opportunity to dream again. How? I'm glad you asked. I decided to pursue my passion as an Actress! I'd always excelled in drama while attending High School, won many awards at state and national level competitions. However, I unfortunately allowed outside influences to deter me from my passion which led me to never have the courage to pursue it as a career.

Now here I am as an adult revisiting a passion that never went away. I didn't know how to start, but my soul needed a dream to work towards and hold on to. I knew eventually it would work itself out. I was scared as hell, don't get me wrong! However, I promised myself that what I was suffering and would eventually overcome, would not be in vain. God will sometimes bring forth our greatest calling from our deepest pain. Acting became the escape of my cruel reality, an outlet to process my pain. I could embody a character and I was no longer myself. For that time, I wasn't me, my problems didn't exist and that allowed me to feel free, even if for a moment. Little did I know, not only would acting put me on a path of healing but also it would breathe hope into my tired soul once again, and Oh, how I needed that!

V.I.V.A—*INSPIRATION*

I want to inspire people. I want someone to look at me and say because of you I didn't give up – Author Unknown

Merriam Webster's definition of Inspiration is: "Something that makes someone want to do something or that gives someone an idea about what to do or create." How often in life have we found ourselves in a dark place and the mere act of turning on a positive YouTube video, read a good book or have an uplifting conversation with someone and boom...our mood changes! It turns on a switch that ignites something in us that allows us to want more, to dream bigger. That is INSPIRATION.

I recall being home many times, depressed when no one knew my circumstances. I would scroll through Facebook. There were no FB lives at the time but there were quotes and videos. People being "vulnerable" and "authentic" wasn't the popular thing to be yet. I saw photos of people's perfect families, promotions at work, bragging about their children or photos of their last getaway, or vacation. Life seemed so perfect for everyone else, which obviously is not the truth. I remember thinking, I wish someone would just be real for once and share their pain and struggles so I wouldn't feel so alone. So, what did I do? I added that to the list of things I would do when I was out of my situation. I vowed to be transparent on social media to give people the inspiration and hope that I yearned for so desperately myself. Now, when my abuser was gone, years later it was time. Ok, I had made that vow but how do I really get started and why would anyone care to listen to what I had to say? Who am I for anyone to even care? Not realizing that whatever God has purposed for you, he also has equipped you for.

Many times, we hold ourselves back from taking that first or next step because we feel unprepared, not educated enough or not qualified. Let me tell you that your experience, your life lessons and the fact that you are STILL HERE, is enough to Qualify You! There are people hungry for hope, thirsty for inspiration and waiting on YOU to step into your purpose and the longer you wait to step into it, you are robbing the world of the magic that sits inside of you.

When I finally did my very first FB live sharing my story on January 2nd, 2017, (shout out to social media coach A.J Joiner for pushing me), I realized, it was there all along. My story was an INSPIRATION to others and that empowered me because I realized that through me speaking out, now others felt seen and heard. …. V.I.V.A.- *VOICE!*

"Your voice can change the world." – Barrack Obama

Finding and owning our voice holds so much power and we fail to recognize that at times. In the pursuit of me finding my own voice, unexpected dramatic changes came about. Not only did I become a voice for others who felt invisible but a NEW version of myself began to surface. I began to gain more confidence, saw things with more clarity while also appreciating seeing things from another's perspective. When you can do that, people are inclined to become more open to what you have to say and you can change people's lives. Your voice is meant to bring about change, but first people need to feel you care in order for them to be receptive to you. It's important to remember that many have spent years building walls, protecting themselves. Compound that with the fact that some of them were raised emotionally neglected. Perhaps in childhood, their parents ignored them when opinions were expressed. They were made to feel as if they didn't matter. Sadly, this led to many feeling invisible. Others may have lost their voice when they lost themselves, their identity was attached to their partner. Wrong relationships also strip us of our voice. There are many reasons why, and we can go on forever about them.

At what point, however, do we grow tired of being quiet, of feeling irrelevant, invisible or drowned out by everyone else? It is when you become tired of being sick and tired and that's when you will no longer be silenced! You will rise and trust me that those that once stripped you from your voice will run and hide once you have taken your power back.

Start with a whisper if you are too scared, but whatever you do, speak.

Let your small whispers build up and before you know it, you will boldly shout your TRUTH, and your truth shall set you free and others along with it.

I can recall when there was a time that I wouldn't speak because I felt no one would believe me anyway, but my tears spoke for me, and God heard my every cry. He saw my every tear. There were nights I'd cry myself to sleep when I'd hide in the closet or turn on the shower so no one would hear…..He heard me.

I didn't need to have a voice, for God to hear me. Because when you can't put into words how you feel, when your chest feels like it can't take more disappointment, and you don't have any more tears to shed, God sees you and hears you. His heart breaks when you break. Rest assured my friend as you read this, God has a plan for you and you are not forgotten. I say this to you because maybe life didn't turn out the way you had hoped. I get it. You're not alone. Just know that one day God will use your story to help someone else and you will remember reading this book. Nothing is ever wasted when you put it in God's hands. However, in order to dream again (VISION), to uplift others (INSPIRATION) to help others (VOICE) first we must accept our past and our current circumstances. Also, part of accepting is to forgive others and forgive ourselves... V.I.V.A.- *ACCEPTANCE*.

It's not what I asked for

Sometimes life just slips in through a back door

And carves out a person

And makes you believe it's all true

And now I've got you

And you're not what I asked for

If I'm honest I know I would give it all back

For a chance to start over

And rewrite an ending or two

For the girl that I knew...

She is gone but she used to be mine

Song by Sara Bareilles

The last place in my story I will take you to, that ties the last word of V.I.V.A, is on an early morning in my car once again. This time I sat outside of the Welfare office. I couldn't believe it! There I was, the woman who gave people jobs to feed their children now was not able to feed her own daughter. How does one go from being a successful business owner of multiple businesses to being broke and on the verge of being homeless? He had kept his word that if I left, I would never see a penny for our daughter or myself. To this day, as I write, he has kept his word.

Although many people express disdain towards those that have had to be on Welfare at some point in their lives. Looking at them as if they were too weak to figure it out on their own, I will be eternally grateful to the department of Santa Clara County Social Services for the support I was given during this time. I was diagnosed with complex PTSD, anxiety and severe depression so I was referred to group therapy and a personal therapist. I did this for at least 3 years. I was granted a protective restraining order against my abuser for domestic violence and life was starting over somewhat.

Many people ask women why they stay in abusive relationships and the most common answer is the kids which translate to finances and hardship. I chose freedom and a new life for my daughter and me so here I was completely unaware that it would take longer than I ever expected for things to improve. I would have thought my nightmare was over but it took nearly 5 years of ongoing court battles, of things that even attorneys would scratch their head and say in their 20-30 something years of practice they had never had to deal with such an individual. Although I had left my abuser, he had found a way for the abuse to continue, because now he would use the court system to punish me. This is called "Systematic" abuse. A corrupt Judge only made matters worse. The pleas of my daughter's own attorney ordered by the court, her therapist and my own attorney would fall on deaf ears. The Judge would just turn the other cheek until just a few months ago when she was removed from family court due to many complaints. During these years, I would be in court WEEKLY for years and sometimes 2-3 times a week. Yes, unheard of, and I was like a walking zombie most of the time just reminding myself to breathe. I share this with you because not only was it already difficult enough for me to have survived the marriage but now to have sunk so low that I couldn't even stand on my own two feet because I didn't even know how to start all over. It's like I had been thrown into a deep pit, and the more I tried to crawl out, the more dirt he would throw at me from the top so that I could never come out.

I also questioned God at times asking why so much would happen to me, things I didn't even deserve. In prayer once, I remember His voice came to me, and he said this, "I know you don't deserve it, but where I am going to use you requires all of this for you to have the credibility for others to hear you out so that people will hear MY compassion through your voice, see ME through your eyes so that they will know that you KNOW their pain, and they will find hope through your story. That's why I need you to go through all of this". A peace came over me and an understanding that what I had faced was never just about me, but about where God was taking me and how HE would use me.

I can't tell you how many people I have sat with, spoken with and others I've never even met that just messaged me via social media because they said they didn't know who else to turn to but they felt they could reach out and trust me. I share this with you because my life certainly didn't end up how I wished: the home, the husband, kids and having my own family. I lost my businesses, my reputation, friendships, relationships and even relatives, and most of all myself. Until I was willing to let go of what could have been, it was when I was able to be open to the new things that would come into my life. I also learned while being at the Welfare office to never judge anyone again. What right do we have?

You never know what someone has been through to end up where they are. I learned to be compassionate and not only accepting past and present but also be accepting of others. I don't know where you are in your journey right now, but I will tell you, "In order to reach for your destiny, you must let go of your history". – Bishop Samuel R. Blakes

Vision   Inspiration   Voice   Acceptance

Today V.I.V.A. continues to grow, soon to be a non-profit. Since sharing my story lives have been touched and transformed locally and even nationally through the power of social media. Viva is a place where your heart can call home. A community of women who through the sharing of their stories, they empower others to help us all find a sense of belonging. Through our quotes, posts, videos, links, FB Lives and events you will find encouragement, strength and hope. We call on the empowered sisters to join us to motivate and inspire other women. We call ALL WOMEN to be a part of us and reach out if you need encouragement. Viva is your voice! As I close this chapter, I invite you to remain open to what the other amazing women that I selected to be a part of this book speak into your life. I ask that you come with no judgment or expectation and consume it like fish- take the meat and throw out the bones. I specifically chose each one of these ladies that are very dear to me and I am blessed to call them friends. Not only do they exemplify what V.I.V.A. is, but I am also confident their stories can heal, inspire, and offer great insight for many of us. As you read, take what is for you and may it bless and propel you to the next level.

Lastly, always remember, you are loved, you are worthy, and your life has a purpose. Despite how bleak your situation may appear at this moment or if you feel your past failures disqualify you, God has a plan for your life. There is nothing impossible for Him, he will meet you at the point of your need because his arm is never too short for you to be out of his reach. You have the potential to become a great leader. You can't have a great leader without great failures and lessons. There is a leader hidden inside of you and trust that God will use the worst of your circumstances for your good and will give you hope and a future to become the leader you were born to be.

Thank you for taking the time to go on this journey with me and I wish you a very fulfilled life always looking to lead and live your life as a V.I.V.A. Woman. That is women who choose to live their life with Vision, Inspiration, Voice, and Acceptance- V.I.V.A.!

Dear Jenn,

When I saw your brother recently, I was excited when we were talking about you and that he also wanted to give you a book. I've always remembered your sweet and kind heart + soul. "Our wounds are often the most beautiful openings into the best and most beautiful parts of us." I hope you enjoy this book and are inspired by our stories. I wish you all the best in your life and you find your joy + peace you wish for.

With love & light,
Elani

ELANI KAY

I Am Exactly Where I Am Supposed To Be

*I*f anyone ever told you that life is supposed to be a smoothly paved road to your best life, they lied to you. I started playing violin when I was four. A very typical thing to do for an Asian American girl I suppose. I started singing and performing solos when I was eight years old. From national anthems to being the lead vocalist of a church worship band, I sang in front of hundreds. In high school, I was in musical theater, dance and mastered music theory. I also played the violin, oboe, and flute. In college, I was a part of an acapella jazz group. Jazz is still a deep love of mine. Music is in my blood. Music is the escape, the peace, the joy, and the fresh air I need every day in my unpredictable life.

During college, I continued my music, but I used to sit in class and think more about this network marketing business I was in and how I was going to make money rather than focusing in class. I was great at converting strangers into friends and then to associates, even though it was super scary for me. I felt very strongly about wanting to be different, and I enjoyed the idea of financial freedom and doing what I love. I worked for two school districts while in college as a para-educator. I was also a discreet trial and applied behavior analysis therapist for autistic children. I loved working with autistic children, even the ones who loved jumping off of everything, especially high places. Life was a lot for me at that time though, and my heart was broken in my personal life, so I was young and a bit reckless, not respecting myself, and eventually I dropped out of college and moved to Hawaii where I lived for about five years. That's when I got hired to work for what is now called iHeartRadio.

Six months after completing my entry-level position my supervisor had left. Everyone had the opportunity to apply for the position, and I jumped on it. I didn't think that out of everyone I would get the promotion, especially with me being so new, but I did! They said my letter was convincing and they wanted to give me a shot. I was so grateful! For the very first time, I was the director of an entire department! I had people that worked for me that were fifteen and twenty years older than me. I felt really bad about it. So bad, in fact, that I lied about my age and I was pretty much 32 years old for an entire decade, even though I was just in my early twenties. Ssssshhh, don't tell anyone.

I learned that I was extremely resourceful and quickly learned on my own how to set up everything while in that position. I would participate in music meetings, conducted group interviews, and went on to direct interns for the promotion departments. I dabbled in almost everything. I learned about sales, marketing, working with record labels, their reps, and even organizing up to sometimes 27 events a week. We had seven radio stations, four FM stations and three AM stations.

I gained a lot of invaluable experience and knowledge. I also went through some tough lessons working in an industry that was high in testosterone and in a place where the rules were much more relaxed. I was the subject of many sexually charged conversations in meetings, on-air, and in person. I was the target of a situation that gave me the right to sue, but I didn't know then that I could. I had to fire a man once who professed his love for me. He cornered me into a studio and I truly feared for my safety but was able to safely get myself out. For months I had people walk me to my car every night. I had to learn to fight for myself and stand up even when I knew what was being said about me behind my back. The workplace was not always safe or fun. There were too many situations to name. I kept moving forward though. I didn't finish college and I was very young, so I wasn't going to just quit and run.

A few years later, life happened, and at 24 years old I became a mother. I had my first son in Hawaii, all alone, away from my family, and it was…extremely hard. Having a child away from your immediate family taught me the value of finding a support system. You find your village, and I did. I acquired friends that are still family today, and they helped me during that time. I was able to bring my baby to work often, but when I was unable to, my close friend, who is now like my sister, would babysit him. I must mention, she would babysit him for free. She called it "parent training" for when she would become a Mom in the future.

When I was fully on my own as a Mother, I vowed to focus solely on my son and my career, but that was short-lived. I was still very naïve, and I fell in love with the idea of being saved by a man. That man and I decided to work towards building a future together and had a love child. After that, I really needed help. Having two kids was too much without family help and the relationship was very unstable. We decided to move back to California, and we moved in with my parents.

I got creative and took on a variety of different jobs. I was teaching and singing. I started a photography business and specialized in photographing kids. Even though all my jobs weren't as corporate as my position in Hawaii I was still doing what I loved. I also took an online business course which led me to take life coaching classes. I found another passion in that process and became a life coach.

I found that when you stay aligned with who you are, God will cause the Universe to align you with people and situations that will give you the opportunity to do more of what your calling is.

This is what happened to me, and I ended up meeting this gentleman who owned an online radio station. From there, we built a partnership and I started creating our marketing team. I had three teams from all over, from the Bay Area and Southern California, and then I went international. I built three teams in six different countries. It was so rewarding and validating to me in terms of what I was able to create and build. We drove traffic to our website and increased the numbers to over 1 million hits a month!

To add to the enthusiasm of life at that time my oldest son was scouted in New York and got signed to a SAG-AFRA franchised talent agency in L.A.! This ended up being a life-changing decision for him, because he booked national commercials, TV Shows, print jobs and worked for very large names like Samsung, Disney Jr., Netflix, Comedy Central, Nike, and more. I would drive back and forth from Northern California to Southern for about a year and a half while working on my international business. It was a huge sacrifice, but he had a natural talent and the desire that I wanted to support. In 2015, I decided to move us to L.A.

When my oldest son was eight years old, we were working on his timeline and he wrote out at sixteen that his goal was to be a millionaire. I "tried" to suggest eighteen, but he was adamant about sixteen. I was like, dang! Mom better get her stuff together! He knew that he wanted to play professional basketball and he wanted to be a famous actor. He was very goal-driven and very specific. He had a work ethic. It was something he chose and not me. He did also mention that one day he'd like to say words that impact other people. He said like Tony Robbins.

I was there to support him on this journey, so we did those drives and went back and forth. I could not have done any of that without the support of my parents. It was a family commitment with all the time away and the boring drives for the younger brothers and all of them waiting in the audition waiting rooms needing to be quiet and well behaved.

We made the commitment to move to L.A. This move was a big sacrifice for me as well. I met another man who learned about what I was doing with the online radio station and felt that I would be a great fit for what he was building in the entertainment industry. I decided to make the move and negotiate my needs which were flexibility to bring my kids to work, being able to work from home at times, and being able to leave at any point to get my son to an audition. Now, I'm back to being on my own, away from immediate family and I was not only a momager, but now I'm also on the other side of learning what it's like to be in production, operating multiple businesses, managing a building, and more. I met a lot of great people through this process. I gave awareness to the face that *everyone you meet should see you as you wish to be seen.* This is probably one of the hardest things I've chosen to try to master because many people seem to have a goal to try to take you out of character, but practicing this has helped me with my personal discipline and having power over my own peace of mind. It also meant when I needed people to see me stand in my power, I showed them that person as well.

This part of my path was still following my alignment philosophy, because these moves would serve a greater purpose later down the road. I, of course, could not elevate though without the hardships and life's greatest lessons being revealed through them. We all must face ourselves and conquer our own inner wounds at some point. While everything seemed to be great with so much opportunity, I chose to not complain but to just take action. It was tough though because my youngest one was still in diapers. I would be at the office and changing diapers and running two full operations and managing my son's career, while also dealing with caregiving. On a daily basis, the one I was caregiving for was extremely verbally abusive. While I was in meetings I would be receiving one text after another threatening over my life or reminders of my inability to do anything but perform sexual acts or how worthless and ugly I was.

This was not a person I could just abandon, because he had nowhere else to go.

Out of everything I was doing, the toughest part was dealing with the constant daily verbal, mental, and emotional abuse that came in the form of texts and emails day in and day out. I wouldn't find myself able to admit the physical part of the abuse until writing this piece. This had been going on for five years. Just hearing my phone go off would make my heart rate go faster and palms filled with sweat. I was keeping it all composed, but inside I was really struggling. I was advocating for this person as well. I was trying to help them get better and help them get the services and support they needed. I was doing all that while pursuing my own personal goals. I did accomplish working with a local congressman and pushing through the evidence with support for their office to make some big changes in policy surrounding the issue we were fighting for to get the help we needed as well as help others. They sent my data to Washington and years later, I saw the changes implemented. I hope to this day that what we both endured was a part of what needed to happen to help save other lives and prevent what happened to us for others.

I did get to a certain point in time where I had to get a restraining order and criminal restraining order from this person after we no longer were in communication. This person wanted me dead. This person still wants me dead. I had spent too many years running and hiding in motels, leaving the state, and being forced to not feel free because of fear. I could not care more about this person than myself and my children any longer. I had to go to court. Protecting your peace of mind must be a priority, which I had neglected to choose for too long. I first went to the police after a specific outburst had occurred. I never liked using the word "victim," but in the eyes of the court, I was the victim. This was very challenging, but also a time where I needed to practice self-control. I would remind myself that *if the ocean can calm itself, so can I.* One of the most important truths about life that I learned from this is that *life is about how you react to it and not so much about what happens to you or for you, it's all about your reaction to what is happening in your life.*

Two weeks after I testified, I spoke at the Business Expert Forum at the Harvard Faculty Club at Harvard in front of doctors, CEOs, financial experts, and professionals. The ultimate blessing for finally letting go was that after I shed the negative energy that was attached to me, it was like I stepped into my skin completely. I stepped into my destiny, my purpose because my purpose and passion were always just to help other people.

I realized that I couldn't forsake all these other lives that were waiting for this message, for the platforms, for the inspiration and for me to help them because of this one person. I continued to move forward. I would also be reminded of the phrase to '*enjoy each moment,*' all the time, but I didn't truly understand this until I regained the freedom to live life on my terms. I even co-authored 3 books. Two international best-selling books!

Life didn't simply become easy though. I was juggling all these obligations while going to court to testify. It was one of the most traumatic experiences of my life. I had to sit on the stand, speak into this microphone in front of strangers and this person. I had to depict details of what happened to me, the threats that were made on my life, personal things, and repeat horrific things said about me. I would leave the court and walk right into meetings happily interacting with professionals. It was difficult to have to transition from reliving experiences as a victim in court then stepping outside and having to be an independent professional woman with no breaks to allow my mind to wrap itself around it all. I had my three young children, who are now thirteen, eleven, and seven, but at the time were younger.

When you live with negative energy for so long and are able to get rid of it, you experience a feeling of rejuvenation, like breathing fresh air, and it was that feeling that fueled my energy to juggle all of the responsibilities.

Through divine intervention, synchronization, my faith, and being resourceful, and, once again, staying aligned to who I was, God brought me many people- my village. I was blessed to live in a home, and I opened my doors up to different people. I was an admin of a group that supports families that have children that want to be in the entertainment industry, so a lot of these parents would bring their kids to stay in my home before their auditions for the encouragement. It forced me to be positive and I would not have to be alone in my house with just the kids.

I had the support I needed. So many angels as I call them came into my life. They are all still supporting me along my journey which I am so grateful for. One woman who is older than me, she's now sixty and a chaplain, is now a real part of our family. Through her, I had the power of prayer and someone that was truly spiritually strong to be there for me. Then I got a dog, Rocky. He was a big fluffy Husky. I was dog-sitting for a friend who could not have the dog in her house at the time and this dog was an awesome watchdog. My first time ever having a dog, so I felt safe which was exactly what I needed. We now have our own dog in our family, a pit bull named Milli.

I thought the cycle of abuse had ended, but I quickly found that it showed up in the professional area of my life, and with it, I learned the power of discernment. The power to say "no" in order to keep my peace. I learned to protect my peace of mind first. I learned how to navigate my way through new situations and important paperwork that I never had dealt with before.

When you're creating something that you've never created before, you have to learn as you go, and you'll make mistakes, you'll be taken advantage of, but the important part is to learn from them. To guard myself I unconsciously put up many blocks after so many traumatic events and that rejection of energy also included the good stuff. I had to re-learn how to receive it again. From compliments and even help, I had to re-program that I was worthy of receiving. I called it 'exercising your receiving muscle,' and this is something I've tried to teach others to learn how to exercise that receiving muscle as well.

To accomplish big goals, you'll have to make big moves. It will feel uncomfortable and scary, but you must move forward anyway. There were so many firsts for me and so many things that I never thought that I could do. I learned how much "more" my self-belief needed to grow. With my business, I wanted to be able to provide as many platforms as I can for other people to get their message out, and so now I have that! People can create content, film, conduct photoshoots, make music, record podcasts, and more.

I also co-own a talent management company. I now have people that I can trust and that I want to grow with around me, because their objective is like mine, to help more people using the businesses and the platform that we create. *You are the average of the 5 people you spend the most time with. Mentally, emotionally, and spiritually surround yourself with who you want to be like.* This was key to my growth as a businesswoman. Based on my past experiences of coming across people that I couldn't trust, it didn't make me fearful of moving forward and not believing that I could ever trust again, it made me more prepared and wiser.

Life experience, support, and faith, along with learning the life coaching tools, all led me to be able to trust again, to have faith, to love again, and to do many things that many people would be afraid to do after what happened to me. Through my life coaching, I've wired my subconscious mind to believe that all things are possible and to look at situations from a positive standpoint, and through this, I want to help as many people as I can personally and through others and to inspire and motivate. *Nothing is ever permanent, so why create permanent emotions off temporary situations?*

I've learned how to become very aware of the thoughts that I have, my self-talk, and when I catch myself saying in my head negative, fearful, and words of doubt, I immediately stop it and turn it around. *Self-actualization and awareness of my inner dialogue have been a significant tool that I used to elevate myself when life tried to knock me down.*

Anything is possible with the power of belief in yourself, but first, you must focus on why you want it so that you can keep your eyes on that when it gets tough. Create your "why" on how it will serve others, and zone in on that "why" with laser focus and declare it to the world that it shall be done. Claim it, just allow, and it will come to be. Remember, nothing is permanent. This is the golden rule. When anything, even life, and death situations occur, remembering this can save the moment and propel you forward to the life you choose. Live and lead by showing, not just saying. It takes action to make things happen, so push through your fears, do it anyway and find your own melody of life.

MELINDA KATE

The Ripples

I was born into happiness, made for love and destined for greatness. I was born with value and worth. I wasn't born frustrated. I wasn't born disappointed or broken. None of us are. We are just born. Then the ripple effect of our lives begins.

I grew up in a house full of love from two loving parents, surrounded by siblings, the second born of my mother and father. My older sibling, my sister, was just like my mom. We grew up playing "kick the can" outside in a very safe neighborhood, where we ran the streets. We played Charades with all kinds of costumes that my mom had made, and I had the greatest job- the kitchen. When it was my night to clean the kitchen, I organized and scrubbed the edges of the sink and faucet. I wiped down the cabinets and I organized the fridge.

I wanted to prove myself as the best of my parents' 5 kids, and I took great pride in doing what I did. I got straight A's as a student. I brought home that report card proudly, my parents would reward me $5 for an A, $4 for a B, and $3 for a C. I always aimed to do my best. So, I did whatever I could do to prove myself as a daughter, to stand out as a young woman. I grew up with such an amazing childhood, and all I wanted to be was a wife and mom, just like my mom. Part of me deep down thought, "I'm going to do it even better than she did."

I was a leader in the youth group. I was a singer in the church. And this vision of being a wife and a mom, it just grew, because my childhood was awesome. As a singer and young lady on the worship team at church, I was up there on the stage, and I'll confess, I scanned the room looking for potential boyfriends and a husband.

I was like, "This is my destiny, and I have to find the right guy. He is out there, and I'm up here, and he's going to find me, and I'm going to find him." I would scan the sea of faces, just trying to catch somebody's eye. I felt confident about who I was. I looked like I was in my early twenties, yet I was a teenager. And I thought, "Ooh, I'm proving myself as a young woman. I'm going to really make it. I'm doing great."

As time went on, so did the ripple effect of my life. The ripples just kept going out, even though I didn't know they were. That's what happens. It's like throwing a pebble into a puddle of water, and the ripples just start to happen. The pebble doesn't know it, the ripples don't know it, yet we can see it. Every one around can see it.

Well, I finally saw somebody in the audience, and he caught my eye. After worship, he came to where I was serving in the kid's ministry. See, I was already practicing being a mom. I was taking it seriously. So, I was in there, and he peeked over and started talking to me. The flirting began, and so did the ripple effect of who I was becoming.

We're always becoming, and I was becoming; that ripple effect was happening. Little did I know that he was 12 years older than me. I knew he wasn't my age, and I knew he was talking to me as if I was an older woman, yet this validated what I was trying to accomplish. What I was trying to prove is that I'm strong. I'm brave. I'm above the maturity of the other girls my age, and I'm going to make it to the status that I desired in my life.

This relationship began offline, through older friends from the youth group. I believed, living in my parents' home as a 15-year-old girl, that this relationship wasn't going to progress into anything serious. I couldn't even date anybody without my parents' permission. I wasn't supposed to do that until I was 16. This was before cell phones and all the advanced technology that we have these days, so there was limited communication.

Little secret meetings began to happen through friends, and I thought, "Oh, this is mature, this is cool. Especially since my parents aren't in the know about it. It must mean I'm able to take on more adult kinds of things." The relationship continued, and I didn't fully understand what was happening.

As I came to know him better he started telling me his story. He spoke about another young woman that he so desperately loved, who had been torn away from him because he was way older than her. The law had taken him away from her and separated them. He went to jail, and this horrible love story that had been broken apart began to press on my heart.

All I thought to myself was, "Man, I wish I could be talked about by someone the way he talks about her. I wish I could be wanted like that or missed like that or valued like that." I began to create a fantasy for myself that I wanted to be her. I wanted to be with him, or I wanted to soothe that ache that he had for her.

As time continued, he slowly began drawing me further and further in. In my mind, the fantasy was coming true. I thought, "Wow, even though he's 12 years older than me he wants to be with me." As I had grown in the church and been taught from my parents; I was to "respect your elders". I believed he had something to show me. I believed I could learn from him. I didn't fully comprehend how dangerous that situation really was.

One night I was with him while a friend vouched for me. Other nights we would find places to kiss and make out in his red Mazda Miata. This one night, in particular, he drove me to my bank, leaned over to me in the passenger seat and asked me for my card and bank account passcode to get money. He drew money out of my account, as him being older, I trusted him.

I trusted that he knew what he was doing, and I didn't even ask. I didn't know. I didn't listen to that voice inside of me. I hadn't been taught to have a voice. He then drove to a hotel nearby. As he drove into the parking lot, he asked me, "Do you want to go in there?" I thought to myself and answered, "Yeah, sure. I would really like to kiss you standing up, without having to hide in your car or someplace".

I was a virgin. I didn't know these things, yet, I didn't stop to think, "Wow, he's 12 years my elder, and he's not a virgin." So, I just thought I was going to act strong enough, brave enough, and mature enough. There's no way I was going to be the young 15-year-old girl who didn't know what was going on. Because somewhere deep down, I did know. It was my choice. I was there with him.

We went up the back stairway to the hotel room, and as soon as we went inside, he locked the door and turned the TV on, loudly. He looked outside the window, closed the curtains, and he turned to me. The terror then began. He didn't even take the cover or sheets down from the bed. I began to separate myself from my body. From the ceiling of the room, I watched him take my virginity from me and saw more blood of my own than I had ever seen before.

When it was all said and done, his white t-shirt was covered in my blood. He was mad and frustrated. I felt so dirty and in deep trouble because he had to throw away his white t-shirt in the hotel trash can. I felt like I was leaving evidence behind. I so badly wanted to take it and burn it. Yet, I had to leave it there, covered in my blood. He then called me the name of the young lady he had gone to jail for previously. He began to tell me what my body was going to go through, and what I was going to feel. He began to instruct me as to what the next days would be like because he knew I was a virgin. Again, it was this sense of, "He's older, and he knows how to do this, and I am to follow him and obey."

I left there with a secret that I was going to tell no one. I was going to be mature, brave and intelligent enough to handle it. This is what I had chosen. I believed I had to remain in my choice. The fantasy grew and I believed I had to make this man become my husband. After all, I had vowed and promised to never have sex with anyone except my husband. I remember coming home that night, sitting on my knees looking at my purity ring on my left hand... and weeping.

That dream of being a wife and a mom–this was now how I had to make it happen. I clung to him. I tried to create this future with him, all in secret; to run away. I communicated with him through a pager he had given me, and with 143 pager codes, he'd want me to call him back when I was alone. It felt so secretive and grown-up.

The more I was clinging to him and the vision of the future I wanted to create, the more he steadily disengaged. That made me want to try harder. I needed to correct my choice. This had to be my future. No one was to know what happened. Little by little, he pulled away. Then on Halloween 1997, the fantasy that I was building all came crashing down. It was Harvest Festival at my church. My dad drove the trailer cart that had hay bales in it. All the kids would sit on them, and he'd drive around as their giggles went up into the crisp fall night air.

I was the only young person there that wasn't laughing and enjoying candy or participating in the games with the others. I sat there knowing this older man who knew my secret was on the other side of the parking lot. I had no idea he was going to confess what he had done, what we had done. He wanted to confess because he wanted to be rid of me.

He didn't know how else to do it. He confessed that night to my dad, and to the church leadership. He had stolen my virginity, and I was now no longer hiding. Everything was out, and I was no longer by myself in this darkness; yet, I desperately wanted to stay there because I didn't think it was darkness. I thought, "This is what I had chosen. I'm a big girl. He didn't do anything wrong, and I am not a victim." That's the tune that I'd play in my head for the next couple of years, that he didn't do anything wrong.

I defended him. I defended the offender who caused a disruption in the ripples of my life. I was born with value and worth, yet I was blinded to it. The ripples of that obliviousness continued for many years until the next splash of events disrupted my life taking those ripples in a new direction. A new pebble was thrown into my life, and I didn't even recognize what had happened.

34

I wasn't taught and I didn't know. Twenty years later I finally realized that I had been digging myself further and further into a pit. I thought if I just dug harder if I was smarter, if I was prettier, if I was more successful, I could get myself out of this dark pit of my life story that had led up to that moment.

My parents had taken me to get counseling, yet the counselors left the room frustrated because they couldn't get through to me. I'd become a hard fortress with the 15-year old me protected behind the walls. I was hiding, and I wanted to prove myself on my own, even though everything had been exposed. Now 20 years later, I was finally able to recognize

my reality because I had a new defining moment. A new pebble had been dropped in the ripple of my life.

I had gotten a husband. I had become the mother of three sons. The defining moment of divorce burst into the puddle of my life with devastating boulder size magnitude. I was a pastor's wife, and I had everything I ever thought I wanted, and I had it all without having to deal with what had happened to me when I was 15. I thought I could erase it, and it would go away because I have this great life, three kids, a pastor's wife, and even my dream as a worship leader!

I found myself going through a divorce, leaving me to feel unwanted again! My ministry was disappearing, and I had no place to call home. Once again, I was exposed. That defining moment was my reality, and I couldn't hide it in marriage or anywhere. "I'm a divorced woman." That defining moment set me on a course to better myself, to find the voice I had lost when I was 15, and to reprogram my mind so that I could change my thoughts in order to change my life. I needed to throw a new pebble in my own puddle and create a new ripple, one where I was the author. I began the journey of personal development.

I found myself single with three boys, eighty pounds overweight and carrying baggage that I didn't even know how to identify. I found ways to get free counseling. As a stay at home mom, I searched out opportunities. I had no college degree. I had no job. My ex-husband held all the cards.

The day before our divorce was final, both lawyers said to me, "You are not going to make it. You're going to end up homeless. The best bet you have is to stay married to this guy. He's not that bad. Drink a bottle of wine every night before you sleep with him."

Both lawyers on either side agreed with this proposition. They said, "You have no plan. You have no future. You have no education. The best thing you can do is to stay with this man." And I thought about it for a moment, that I could stay with him, use him for his money, get an education. Then leave him. I chose not to do that. I chose not to do that to myself, my sons, or their father.

Instead, I resolved, "I'm going to make it. I don't know-how, yet I am going to do the right thing for my life, and I'm going to make it." I put myself into counseling. I looked at programs. I began to better myself as much as I could, get out of debt, create a life, and get on a path to becoming independent, strong, brave, and the dominating force of my own life.

STAND

I consciously made the choice to take personal responsibility for what I COULD DO instead of saying, "This is the bed I made, and now I have to sleep in it." I began to look at, what CAN I do? What do I GET TO do? What IF things went a different way? What IF I could control the ripples of my life? I stood up in the pit that I had been digging. I got up off those dirty knees, and I stood. "STAND Melinda Kate STAND!" I then looked up. I was able to recognize who had been throwing dirt on me this whole time I'd been trying to dig a way out.

LOOKUP

Once I shielded my eyes from the dirt being thrown on me, I begin to see and hear others extending a hand down, calmly saying, "Look at that root right there. Grab onto that root. Look at that step. Put your foot right there. You can get out of this mess. LOOK UP Melinda Kate LOOKUP. Listen to the sound of my voice. Here's a rope. Pull yourself out." And so, my relentless escape efforts were redirected! I was set on getting out of this pit.

YOU'RE WORTH IT

With each step, my confidence grew, and I began to trust myself. I'd look up and grab, step up, and hear the voices gently calling me out of this pit. YOU'RE WORTH IT Melinda Kate YOU'RE WORTH IT. I saw the light at the end of the tunnel, and I said, "I'm running for it." I was able to get my life on track, get out of debt, and with a positive community, a personal coach, and program; lose those eighty pounds! And I've kept it off for three years!

> *"If you fall, fall on your back. If you can look up, you can get up."*- **Les Brown**

I created a whole new life for myself because I found a career in coaching others in similar steps of healing, transformation, and freedom. Being a Transformation Coach or *Hope Dealer* allows me to stay home with my boys, work remotely, travel, and never miss a moment with them. I learned how to give myself everything I have been looking for in another person.

It's that bright light at the end of the tunnel that gave me just the right amount of hope needed. I found the rope someone was throwing down because I stood up and I looked up. My friends, we are not born overwhelmed. We are not born into dysfunction. We are just born. The ripples of life begin. We don't even know what's happening. We are just here, and then life happens.

I grew up in a great family, in a sheltered home, yet life still happened. It caused the direction of my life to go in a way that I had not predicted, nor wanted. The ripples of trauma, sent me on a course: relationship after relationship, staying loyal in situations way too long that I was never intended or meant to be loyal in.

I've been on this journey of healing and creating a life that is important to me. I've been on this journey for five years of personal growth, healing and development. What if I could have taken that defining moment, and put it 20 years prior? Right at that exact moment where that first pebble was thrown in, and where the new ripple started? What if there was someone reaching down encouraging me, "Don't hide in that pit. Keep looking up. There's a way out of what just happened."

Today, that's what I get to do as a Transformation Life & Business Coach. I get to come into someone's life and offer that pattern disruption; instead of them hiding and trying to dig themselves out of a pit that was never meant for them to be in alone. We are better together.

I've learned so much in these last five years. I wanted to run fast towards being a wife and a mom, and I did exactly that. I ran fast and alone in my own strength and knowledge. As the African proverb says, "If you want to run fast, run alone. If you want to run far, run together." In these last five years, I have run together with people that believe in me and see my worth. People that say, "Stand. Look up, You're worth it."

No matter your age or place of life, if it's not the road you intended, simply remember, " You don't have to. It's not about should, it's not about the need to. It's about, you get to." My friend, your life is not fixed. You get to choose. Others don't choose for us. *You get to be the dominating force of your life, yet it comes to a decision–that defining moment.*

I take very seriously with great joy being the person who reaches my hand down to someone in a pit. Whether someone is in their teenage years, the early twenties, thirties, fifties, or even later in life, I invite you to consider, at this very moment, you are one decision away from a totally different life. It would be my greatest joy and delight to connect with you and hear your story. Together we can discover your new life-defining moment. What are the ripples now, and what do you want it to be? Please connect with me on Facebook, Melinda Kate Gillette, also on Instagram at melindakatemomboss. Please email me at melindakate27@gmail.com.

As I wrap up our time together in these pages, my desire is to provoke you to decide with this final powerful short story that has brought great value to my own journey. May you find healing in these words:

Once upon a time, a woman moved to a cave in the mountains to study with a guru. She wanted, she said, to learn everything

there was to know. The guru supplied her with stacks of books and left her alone so she could study. Every morning, the guru returned to the cave to monitor the woman's progress. In his hand, he carried a heavy wooden cane. Each morning, he asked her the same question: "Have you learned everything there is to know yet?" Each morning, her answer was the same. "No", she said, "I haven't." The guru would then strike her over the head with its cane.

This scenario repeated itself for months. One day the guru entered the cave, asked the same question, heard the same answer, and raised his cane to hit her in the same way, yet the woman grabbed the cane from the guru, stopping his assault in midair. Relieved to end the daily battering yet fearing reprisal, the woman looked up at the guru. To her surprise, the guru smiled. "Congratulations", he said, "you have graduated. You know now everything you need to know."

"How's that?", the woman asked.

"You have learned that you will never learn everything there is to know," he replied. "And you have learned how to stop the pain"."— Melody Beattie

> *TOGETHER, we can stop the pain! I invite you, my friends. Stand and lookup. You're worth it.–* Melinda Kate Gillette

MIA AMOR

Resiliently Embracing
New Beginnings

*I*n recent decades, immigrants have been looked at negatively. Today, I'm proud to be a part of changing the stigma. I was born in El Salvador and am the youngest of three children. My parents met at a young age and quickly married. My mother was already a single mom to my older sister, Jasmine. In the late 80s, my parents decided to flee El Salvador because of the civil war. They wanted to feel safe and live better lives with more opportunities.

Five years later, my parents divorced, and once again my mother found herself as a single mother raising three kids on her own. Despite the fact that she was in a different country and experienced extreme pain and trauma from the physical and verbal abuse by my Dad, she persevered. She focused on making a living off her personal passion as a florist. She is still successful in her business in Silicon Valley.

I have two older siblings, Jasmin and Jose. My sister, Jasmin, is also a florist; she has the same talent as my mother, and they are both in business together. She gave me two amazing nephews who I love so much. I hope this chapter inspires them to reach high levels. My brother, Jose, is a United States Marines veteran. My brother served our country twice and I consider him a very brave and strong soul. He is married and has two kids as well. Unfortunately, I haven't had a relationship or spoken to my brother for the last 10+ years because of certain misunderstandings.

My mother is my biggest inspiration, mentor, best friend and that's who I get my work ethic from. I admire my mother's strength because even though she faced many obstacles she stayed strong, fearless and led with love. She is very talented at her craft. My mom started her business by selling flowers at local bars and nightclubs. She set up flower stands on the street corners and grew it to eventually have a storefront flower shop. She's known as "La Senora de las Flores". Growing up, we would help my mom sell flowers. I used to hate it. I just wanted to hang out with my friends. This was how we made a living. My mom worked hard to keep a roof over our heads and provide food, clothing, and shelter. I didn't have a normal childhood like most kids. We didn't travel much or go on family vacations. The first time I went to Disneyland was in 2018 and that was through a radio promotion. We struggled a lot and we didn't have much growing up, but we sure had love within our family and my mother always made sure of that.

I ALWAYS KNEW WHAT I WANTED

I grew up on the east side of San Jose, California, in a Latino neighborhood. We moved a lot which made it easier to adapt to change, but I always had drive and vision. I knew at a young age that I wanted to be in front of an audience. I was interested in the arts.

I remember in elementary school I wanted to sing and be a performer like Selena Quintanilla. In the 4th grade, I remember walking by the band classroom and hearing all the instruments playing. I walked in, interrupted the class, and literally pointed at the trombone and told the teacher I wanted to play. She said they only had one instrument left, so she had me fill out paperwork and bam! I was on my way to learning and exploring my passion for music. I performed solos, attended Jazz camps, and loved every moment.

In middle school, I continued to play alongside my best friend, Melissa, who played the flute. We had so much fun. I think those were some of my best memories besides rollerblading and hanging with friends. I knew what I wanted at a young age and that drive, and passion never went away.

There was a period in my teens where all I did was go out to clubs, cruising, drinking, smoking, and literally doing nothing productive. I used to hang out with a group of girls who really had no vision for the future. When we went out, we would see the "radio station party crew" and we were excited to talk with them and get free stuff. I appreciated those times because it was all part of my journey to where I am now. God works in mysterious ways. He puts all the signs in front of you without noticing until you open your eyes.

I quickly got tired of hanging with those girls and one day I called them and said I didn't want to be their friend anymore. I was so over it. I know I hurt some feelings because a couple of us were very close. But like I said, I've always had a vision of where I wanted to be, and I wasn't letting anything get in the way of that. It wasn't where I wanted to be, and I wasn't afraid to make a change.

YOU MUST BE CLEAR ON WHAT YOU WANT
AND THE UNIVERSE WILL DELIVER

At the time, I was working part-time at a chiropractic office and I always got in trouble for playing my favorite radio station. There is one specific day where I remember looking at the radio and saying, "I wanna do exactly what that person on the radio is doing." I wanted to be a voice for my community. I wanted to inform people about music, news, and pop culture. That is when everything made sense to me. I quickly enrolled at the local community college because they had a radio and TV broadcasting course. They taught us how to read commercials, how to be an announcer, radio programming, and how radio stations make money. After you proved yourself, they allowed you to be on air for the local campus radio station. I totally tanked my first shift. I was nervous because I had called my mom and sister to tell them I was going to be on. That was embarrassing. The program also offered an internship at a local radio station. I jumped on that opportunity immediately because I knew that was going to be the beginning of my journey to my goal.

I started my radio career in San Francisco as an intern/promo tech. My job was decorating clubs, setting up all events, talking to listeners, going on van hits, and promoting the station. It was so much fun but a lot of work. I lived in the south bay and the station was in San Francisco, so it was a long drive, but I didn't care.

I met some amazing people there that I am still friends with. I used to sneak in and answer phone calls for some of the part-time on-air personalities and they would school me on how it all worked. I was told by one of my mentors that if I wanted to make it in the industry, I had to be comfortable with change and relocating. It was clear that I wasn't going to make a lot of money in the first couple of years until I gained some experience. Of course, I proved myself. My mentor always told me, "You need to start practicing your craft. You need to start pretending and recording airchecks, AKA demos, so you can hear yourself and get comfortable with your voice and delivery." I soaked up all that knowledge. Any advice anyone gave me, I would take it and run with it. Nothing will be handed to you. You must get out there and seek opportunity. I've always had a great personality. I wasn't afraid to talk to program directors and general managers. I was friendly to everyone.

QUICK STOP

I quickly made the move to Salinas, California, to work for KDON as a Promotions Lead, AKA: a van driver. At first, I was hesitant because it was a small market compared to San Francisco. I felt like nothing was going on there, but I knew that I had to relocate and get uncomfortable so I could be more comfortable in the future. Even though I didn't like it, I still did the job commuting from Milpitas to Salinas every other day. I was only employed four months, because I had talked to a local publication about a fight at a Mac Dre concert and my words were misinterpreted. I should have never opened my mouth and commented on that matter, but I did, and ended up getting let go. It was a very big lesson for me.

I'M ON TO THE NEXT ONE

I quickly called my friend Josser and told him the news. He told me he had a friend, Carlos Pedraza, who was looking for a promotions assistant back in San Francisco. It was a new Spanish radio station that was going to be launching soon so I called to apply, had an interview, and they hired me. At first, I was like… Spanish radio? I never imagined myself working on Spanish radio. I am bilingual and proud of my roots. It was something different and that's what I needed at that time. I was open to the opportunity. I needed to get the experience one way or another I was doing pretty much the same thing–going on van hits promoting the radio station, but then quickly got promoted to Promotions Coordinator which had me in the office assisting the promotions director. I did the scheduling, managed the entire team, covered shifts, assisted the promotions director with ideas, and handled pretty much all the execution. I also faced some challenges. I was consistently disrespected and put down by certain male colleagues. It was a problem to their ego that I was in that position. I was accused of sleeping my way up! Those are lies haters make up when they feel intimidated. That didn't stop me because, I knew my truth. That's what you always must tell yourself when others speak wrongly of you, "The truth about me is…"

I've worked alongside some of the biggest on-air personalities in Spanish radio and one woman that stood out to me was a strong talented woman we called "LA BRONCA." We became friends quickly and she was killing it on-air and on-stage; she was fierce and so confident. She was one of my inspirations in radio. She would give me advice about entertainment and how you must have thick "skin" especially as a woman and work twice as hard.

I knew then how much I wanted to pursue my on-air radio career. But I had a long way to go! Working as a Promotions Coordinator at the time was no longer fulfilling. I was exhausted all the time. I wasn't happy. If it's not fun anymore, let it go. If it doesn't feed your soul, let it go. You'll be happier working towards what you want in life rather than settling for less.

IT'S NOT WHAT YOU KNOW, IT'S WHO YOU KNOW

That saying is so true! But the good thing is that I did know a little something by then. I was really good at networking and keeping in touch with people in the industry. I quickly learned about a new format entering the radio world on the west coast know as "Hurban" radio. That's when reggaeton was taking over the airwaves.

The station La Kalle needed weekend on-air personalities at the time and since I had met the operations manager at a party I attended several weeks back, I emailed him my demo. I had no real on-air experience but knew it was time to stop working behind the scenes. It was time for me to really focus on my goal of being an on-air personality.

I wasn't afraid to take on this new role because I knew what I wanted and consistently reminded myself that, "I could do this." The OM ended up loving my aircheck and put me in contact with the Program Director who loved my vibe because I could do the whole "Spanglish" delivery on-air and that's what they were looking for. I jumped on the weekend shift and ended up making decent money to pay my bills and commute to the south bay. I did club gigs for extra money. I wasn't the best at my craft back then, but I didn't care. Every opportunity I had to rock the mic, I did it and got better with time.

When you're focused on your passion the universe opens doors you never expected. That's what happened next. I received a phone call from my mentor who was working in Salinas at the station I had gotten fired from four years before. They had an overnight position available, but I also had to do the production. It sounded perfect. The only problem was, I had to move. I had no family there, just a couple of people that I knew from before. This was my first full-time on-air job and I was ready to walk in with vengeance through those hallways.

How do you say my name in Spanish? MIA AMOR

The show they offered me was an overnight slow Jamz, love dedications show that played R&B and love songs. They called it "Night Moves." OMG! It was the best show to have. My program director at the time was thinking of a name that I could use on-air. Since people already knew me as Mia he asked how you say my love in Spanish? "Mia Amor"–and boom it stuck. He changed the Jay-Z lyrics a little, but it sounded the same and it went with the whole theme of the show–Night Moves with Mia Amor. That's basically the story of how I got my radio name. I did the show for seven months and then a midday position from 10:00 AM to 3:00 PM opened up.

You know, I had been slowly but surely paying my dues, so I was the first person they felt needed to be promoted. I was grateful for the opportunity and DAMN EXCITED!

Some people didn't have my best interest and that's the reality of this business. People will talk about you, critique you, hate on you, and speak lies. For a period, the hate was real. I had to keep my eye on the prize and keep positive and recognize what was real. I found that in my best friend Samantha who I met working there. Samantha and I are still friends to this day. She was my support system. There were many lonely, sad nights. My family was away and didn't visit as much as I wanted them to. They did their best.

During this chapter of my life, I learned about depression. I was still very young and learning every day. I ended up being promoted to Promotions Coordinator and once again I was working alongside the sales department. I was on-air and still working very long hard hours. I was much happier because I was growing. People there trusted me, but one day I took advantage of that trust. I took the station vehicle out and drove it for my personal benefit. I ended up getting a DUI in the station vehicle and I lost everything that I had worked so hard for. To this day, none of my family members know this happened, but my truth is coming out today. I was so torn apart I didn't know what I was going to do to get back on my feet.

At the same time, I had been presented with a big opportunity back in San Francisco at a hip-hop station to fill in for middays because their midday girl who was going on maternity leave. I was so upset people had really started to believe in me, recognize my talents, and then I messed everything up. It had been a Golden ticket for me to be at a major market radio station and I blew it by making that one bad decision.

Later I learned that things happen for a reason, and sometimes bad things happen because we make stupid decisions, but God always finds a way to turn it around to our benefit when he sees that we learned. Part of learning is taking accountability and responsibility for our actions. It's a part of "growing" and learning life's lessons.

I was unemployed for six months, my mom was paying my bills, and I had to move back to the Bay Area. I was trying to figure out what my next move was going to be. I was sending my resume and air checks to different radio stations in different markets. After six months I was presented with two opportunities, one in Sacramento and the other in Las Vegas. The opportunity in Sacramento did not allow me to be in the air. For the second offer, the company flew me out to Las Vegas for the interview and audition. I was soon warned of the turmoil this job came with. I nailed the audition and was offered an overnight position which meant I had to take two steps back just to be back on the radio doing what I love. Before even taking this new opportunity a lot of people told me that it was going to be a rough chapter in my life because the Program Director at the radio station was not a very nice person. But I didn't care. I had to make a move, continue to grow, and so I moved to Las Vegas all alone with no family or friends there.

This was a big high profile move for me, doing overnights at the local hip hop station. I was so nervous to be away from family for the very first time in another state. I couldn't just drive to my mom's house like before. I had no friends, and let me tell you, walking into that building every day was not easy. I felt like I was walking on eggshells every single day.

Some of the people I had made friends with there did not have my best interest. They were jealous and would talk about me. They made fun of me on social media. A lot of people in this industry are very insecure. I get it. Nobody wants their job to be taken away, and in this business, there is a lot of competition. My boss seemed to not like me, and it was a constant challenge to work with her. I was treated so badly. There was no level of respect, just demands. I remember one day my "Program Director" was upset that I slid my show prep under her office door, and she came to the studio to yell at me. She threw the papers at me and yelled. I cried for the first time in the studio that day. The level of abuse in that place was horrible. It took me two years to finally get to a good place with my Program Director. I wondered why she didn't just fire me, but she later confessed that she was happy with my growth so maybe she was going through her own things at the time. There were times, I wanted to give up. I cried at night and missed my family. They didn't come to visit much. My mom took care of my grandmother, so it was challenging. I would fly out to visit them instead.

These are the kinds of challenges you will sometimes face on your journey. It will not always be pretty. I get asked all the time, "How did you get to be on-air?" "By not giving up", I tell them. You cry, suck it up, have thick skin and keep it moving. If I would have quit, then all the hard work I put in would be out the window.

You must surround yourself with good people. I met some great people that are now my extended family. Without them, I don't know how I would've lasted so long in Las Vegas. I hosted clubs, concerts, and interviewed some A-list celebrities. I went from the overnight show to middays, and then morning drive. I was involved with the youth and community.

This company didn't know my worth though. I kept growing but my salary didn't. I was struggling and had to get a part-time job. I felt stuck for a while.

"Know yourself, know your worth, My actions speak louder than my words"- Drake

Soon enough I received a call from San Francisco informing me of a new radio station that was going to launch, and an offer would becoming. I thought this was my big break! I was sad to leave Las Vegas because of all the relationships I had made, and I had settled in nicely, but certain things weren't aligned like I would have liked. Here I go moving again; starting over in a sense. The hardest thing on the radio has been the moving part. It's not been easy for me. But since my family would be around, it felt right.

I had the chance to work alongside some of the biggest on-air personalities in the Bay Area. Many were people who I looked up to growing up and listened to daily. To be surrounded by such big talent was an honor and the best part about it. They knew who I was too and were supporters. That's an amazing feeling. I loved working for the "throwback" format; everything from the 90s and 2000s. They were all the songs I grew up listening to. I was doing almost everything I envisioned myself doing. I felt more confident in my work. I've always been confident but this time it was different. I now felt more stable.

Once again, I went from doing afternoon drive to mornings in market 4 radio. WOW! I still couldn't believe how my life had changed for the better. Doing a show by myself vs doing a morning show and having a co-host had its challenges. It's like being married; you now have a work husband. You don't always agree but you're in it together, so you make it work. I learned a lot from my co-host, Joey Vee, he was talented and organized. The best show-prepper I've known lol. We balanced each other out. We became a family; we cried together, laughed together, and celebrated together. Our morning show was featured in the SF WEEKLY Radio Waves segment. I loved my PD at the time. We would air-check every week consistently and through those constructive sessions, I improved my craft. He was always complimentary and taught me ways I could sound and be better.

I cherish those moments because they allowed me to grow and develop my skills. The Bay Area was really feeling this dynamic duo. I had been there for 4 ½ years when this train made a stop we weren't expecting. I had to face some personal realities. My father was struggling and almost homeless, my mother had suffered a stroke, and I was working full time trying to take care of myself and be supportive. This was a heavy load that led me to depression. I visited a therapist for guidance and healing. I was a different person and a grown woman by now and I needed clarity; life felt cloudy.

I encourage all of you to take care of your mental health. It has changed my way of looking at everything. I no longer carry guilt and pain. I realized that a lot of my pain stems from family and childhood. I'm not ashamed of speaking about this because if we don't do the work on ourselves, we will continue to bleed.

Soon enough, more changes were in the works for me. God always has a plan. His plan was to re-direct me to Sacramento. The company I worked for merged and completely changed the direction I was on. I was laid off and soon enough the news was all over the radio media outlets, and my inbox became full. At one point I said to myself "I made an impact here." I'm glad I get to walk away knowing I fulfilled my purpose. People really support me in the Bay Area, but I was thinking about taking a break from radio since that's all I had focused on literally since I was 18 years old. I never really focused on my personal life. I'm still single and have no kids. I've dated throughout the years but nothing stuck. My life had been changing every couple of years. I was okay with taking a break and that was the plan–but not God's Plan!

I was rehired by the same company in Sacramento 1 month later and was offered my own morning show. Nine months later, my old San Francisco station called and rehired me. I'm now hosting two shows; one in Sacramento and one in San Francisco. I say that with pride.

Through everything that I've accomplished, I've had to find the courage to make decisions alone. I've had to fight through emotions, fear, hard times, loneliness, abuse, haters, and change. I found that it was the struggle that has made me *RESILIENT*! I now know I can get through anything.

With *FAITH*, I would reach higher levels because God intended that for my life. You must *BELIEVE* you can make it. You must *CLAIM IT*. Go fight and get what you want! It will happen in due time. I don't claim to know everything, but I do know my journey and I will share what has worked for me.

Know what you want: I've had many conversations with teens and young adults, and they don't know what they want. They know they want to go to college but once they finish, they don't know what's next. Do some soul searching and find out what you're willing to chase and go after. What will fulfill you? We all have a different assignment in life, find what yours is. I get asked all the time, "How did you start?"

I always answer, "I knew that I wanted to be on-air." I researched and made it happen. I took the steps necessary to get there, no matter the challenges. Sometimes they look at me in disbelief which I think is funny. In their minds, they think I just applied and got hired. It doesn't work that way.

Network: Be courageous and reach out to people you may not necessarily know and introduce yourself. Ask questions, tell them you're a fan, admire what they do, are interested in the same industry, etc.

Always be professional and speak up. Closed mouths don't get fed. Your next job may be an introduction away and you don't even know it. One thing to also keep in mind is to not burn your bridges. Always be professional even when you don't agree with the situation or it doesn't feel right inside. It's OK to say no and move on. The right opportunities will present themselves.

Talent vs. Skills: I heard Will Smith say, "Talent you have naturally, skill is only developed by hours and hours of working on your craft." So take the time daily to work on your skills.

I was hesitant on sharing my story with all the edges and secrets that I've kept tucked away, but God speaks to us through the people he brings across our path and I'm forever grateful for the opportunity I was given for me to scatter the seeds of my pains, struggles, lessons, and wisdom with hopes that it will help another woman.

ROXANNA DUMAS

Achieving The Dreams
Of Resiliency

*H*ow do I begin to tell my story? Do I tell the story of my great grandparents, who I only know through magical realism folk tales like those of Gabriel Garcia Marquez? We actually originate from the same "Buendia" lineage name found in his books. Or do I tell the story of my grandparents, whose dreams were shattered through the cruel joke of destiny, much like everything that happens in their homeland? Or do I begin with my parents, who were the first to come to America to live out their dreams? Through a combination of personal choice and forced patriarchal circumstances, the women of El Salvador had made the decision to break free. They all passed on their dreams of resiliency to me.

I come from a long line of men who had power, money, some had education, and skill but lost it because of their inability to build consciousness and look inside and find a self-awareness of how to change what they were doing wrong. How to not allow traumas they had been through impact not only their personal lives but also those they loved.

They were unable to cope, look inside, put a check on their egos and accept their mistakes, learn and pivot. By the time the men woke up, it was too late. They were either broke, lost their families or dead. That was the legacy for my great grandparent's generation. But there was a shift as time went on with my grandparents and in that family space, some of who didn't like what they saw growing up and the men then decided to elevate their skills or education, rise in leadership and many left their home country.

To me, they were like a mirage because the men in our family who were often successful, had a deep consciousness, but they always existed far away from me. So I never really learned their process and it sparked my curiosity. All I knew was they were smart, successful, and I needed to follow in their footsteps. My father's generation was hard working with amazing survival skills, but there were too many scars that impacted their lives in so many ways. They made sure that they were resilient and continue seeking a better life for themselves and their families. There was a lot of turmoil, but they did not give up. The women on the other hand, in their lives, had no choice but to rise up and survive from my great grandparents experience all the way to my current experience. Some were stronger than others and others took the leadership role to get their mothers, brothers, and sisters back on track.

In some instances, some of the women chose to start their own businesses, learn a trade, get married or do whatever in their space and time allowed for them to grow. The women in my family became relentless to survive and powerful. Despite the many adversities in their home country, most learned from their mistakes and made a choice to not allow finances or men to dictate their lives.

In my personal journey, I begin to question everything. No matter what catastrophe, no matter what trial, I always find a way to get back up and to rise above.

I came from a community that nearly destroyed the native indigenous people of their land. The root of colonization and ongoing violence within two civil wars. That constant thought of danger and survival is always there. It allows me to see the beauty around me more intensely. I appreciate those moments of joy and there is a constant reminder that everything, no matter what, we must continue on. There is a mission to survive despite it all. Being stagnant is not an option for me. We can decide to move on by choice or life will choose it for you.

I was born in San Francisco where diversity was all I knew and the need for constant innovation and integration of all these communities. I was a sponge and I was picking everything up from the good, bad and the ugly. I always wanted to understand the why of everything. I also had to learn to apply all of this resiliency that I learned from my family and heritage. I developed independence through fighting for my rights while living in the Bay area. I was only in fourth grade when this was put to the test for the first time. I distinctly remember when a teacher was upset that I had said that she had a preference for the model minorities and for white students. She really didn't see what she was doing or saying to the rest of us in the classroom that could have caused me to feel this way. She decided to question me in front of everybody in the hallway and say, "You have to apologize for those negative things you said about me."

I looked her straight in the eyes, I don't think I was older than maybe eight or nine years old, and I said, "My mother said that if I don't believe it to be right, that I do not have to apologize," and so I didn't!

At that moment I understood that I had to stand up for my rights to this teacher. I didn't feel that she was treating me fairly because

I wasn't being selected to be an honor student when I had the exact same grades as the rest of the Asian community in my class, and the extracurricular activities. I had to speak up for myself and that was only the first part of applying my learned resilience. What I didn't know at the time was that this would not be the first time or the last. It was only the warmup and the evolution of my ability to stand up for myself.

I used all these experiences to start fueling my vision, inspiration, and passion for life. After multiple experiences of both physical and emotional abuse, I turned to music to help me use my voice and channel my expression. I turned to the arts and became a public speaker. I used my education and my love of the written word to transform all these thoughts that I couldn't understand. I didn't have enough people around me who understood my struggles. Being a young Latina, first-generation born in the United States, and coming from the culture of immigrant communities that surrounded me, I struggled at so many different levels.

Through all the experiences with my family I learned how to be extremely resilient, and I also learned how to run a business as young as eight-years old. I was a translator for my family business. I was doing bookkeeping as well as keeping up with my school while translating for all the new immigrant students that were coming through the door. My house was that place where a lot of immigrant families came to celebrate Christmas for the first time and learn about how to live in the United States. Without knowing it, I was being placed in a leadership position while coaching so many people, whether it was through education or business.

I met a woman who became my music and private teacher when I was 10-years old, whose impact ended up taking all my knowledge and experience that I learned from her mentoring to the next level.

She was instrumental in helping me understand that women's roles could be anything that they wanted them to be. She was the first person that I knew who had seven degrees, spoke seven languages. She would meet with me every day after school and became my free private tutor.

By the time I was 11 years old, I was doing college algebra, learning French and German while learning how to play the piano and truly getting myself ready for the next stage of writing and translating. Being exposed to these different experiences, and to some of the violence in my community, growing up in the Mission was constant conflict and there was a constant challenge for me as a girl. How do I speak my truth, use my voice to speak up as I had been taught?

I moved to El Salvador at age 11. My formative teenage years were spent flying back and forth from El Salvador to the United States. While I was going to school in El Salvador I got engaged in the culture there, and I learned what it meant to be a Salvadorian and American. I'd attend the schools here in the States when I came back as well. So, technically I never really had a vacation and that is when I started understanding diversity in many of its aspects. I was getting culture shock on both spaces. I traveled 12 times with my family by road from San Francisco to El Salvador. Witnessing that migrant trail and the things that happened on the road and the stories that I was exposed to at such a young age really showed me the work that I decided to do. Of course, aligning it back to the root of my family. I wanted to understand. Consequently, there were things that never settled with me.

I moved to El Salvador to live there for the first time. Living there showed me what losing my voice and personal power and independence was really like.

The level of abuse and violence, the lack of protection and really learning to negotiate my own space and power in all of these different spaces, and as a young woman it pushed me to study women in gender studies. And for many that knew me, that was questionable. In fact, Latino leaders would tell me, "Why in the world would you major in that? Why don't you major in something that matters?" What they didn't know is that them just saying those words had made that decision for me immediately, because it did matter to me. It should matter to so many people because it's not just about feminism, which is what the misconception is. It's about seeing everything from a different lens, questioning why we are who we are and how we do certain things. This goes for any gender identification but feminism is using a female's gender perspective.

In my work, it doesn't matter if I'm doing political work, business, social change or health reform, I'm looking at it from a different lens, and how it's impacting all those who are not represented for the most part, including me. Music led me on this journey. I used to be the only woman in the room, so I had to learn to negotiate not only in business but also my safety. I really have taken all these tools and learned to deescalate violence, how to rise above violence and allow diversity and language to help me and others to know our rights. We can all build upon our human values to succeed as a community, but also as leaders in whichever communities we are part of.

Humanitarian values played out in every twist and turn of my life and former relationships, whether they were school culture, health, social justice, or business.

It may seem that I do too much and people often can't figure me out. But I don't worry about other's opinions about me because this is my journey and how it aligns for me. These are the steps I'm going to share with you about resiliency, transformation, and empowerment through *voice, acceptance, inspiration, and vision.*

Voice - Voice is personal power. At least this is how I define it. Just think about the many singers and public speakers that have been kicked out of their countries or some cases even killed, because they dared to speak up. One of my favorite artists who reminded me that women could have a voice without having to be overly sexualized and have an outside message that wasn't just pop lyrics was Mercedes Sosa. Her voice really influenced social movements in her region until this day. Her music is recognized but she had to live in exile for using her power and voice.

Using our voice to speak out about what is really happening. Yet after moments of deep pain, when there's a loss, transformative change or unexpected change we may then lose our ability to make our own decisions. Our voice can become this place where we regain our power. We can also lose it forever if we don't make the right choice to bounce back. I was abused as a child and I remembered distinctly that I lost my voice physically. I thought I was screaming, but in all reality, my voice had been lost and only made sounds inside my head.

It left a void inside of me and since that day, my journey to find my voice and make myself stronger and louder began. Not using our voice is like a slow death that can start by manifesting into other forms like physical illness and it will somehow take its toll. There may be others continuing abuse over you, or your inability to experience joy. The list goes on. Go and find your voice. Write something, sing something or just speak up for yourself like I did when I was in fourth grade. That is the first step to really taking back your power and not being silenced as a lot of our cultures around the world have taught women and oppressed communities to do.

Acceptance - After the loss of personal power or your voice, there is this transitional period if you learn the lessons and survive it, you can thrive. First, you must be willing to accept that what has happened is meant for you to learn and transform in this stage. It is also acceptance of what you do and events in life you do not have control, it is a choice that only you can make on how to move forward. After the grieving period for whatever loss you have had, comes that much-needed acceptance, but it's not passive acceptance. In order to rise above and lead your life and perhaps lead others take active acceptance that this is part of your life's journey.

There must be a release of the pain and the negativity of this thing that is holding you back, and peace and acceptance come to catapult you forward. Others may see this also as forgiveness of self and others. The moment of true healing.

How do you know when it's healed? For me at least it is a moment when I can talk about the situation, think or write about that situation, but it's no longer causing that deep pain. I don't cry or feel angry about it. It just is.

This can be something simple as a mundane workplace betrayal or situation from someone that you trusted that let you down, or something deeper, like a traumatic experience. The point is, acceptance is the key before anyone can truly rise above and lead a stronger life or be a leader in different places in a healthy way.

Inspiration - When you think you can't do more to heal or transform the pain because you have accepted and moved on, one day you wake up your consciousness and realize that there is more.

66

You receive a burst of inspiration for your life's work or the next step that will guide you in the best direction of your life. It is time to allow the muse of inspiration and the lessons learned in those stages of darkness to take you where you have no idea you could go. This is where many find and shift their lives around whether it was after healing from cancer or loss of a child, leaving an abusive relationship, etcetera.

In fact, one tangible example is this V.I.V.A. women's project by Mia Perez, the project founder, who transformed her pain into something healing and beautiful. Not only for herself but for the countless women that V.I.V.A. brings together, and that now is being converted into this book with the collection of stories of women who support the leadership from V.I.V.A. and their participants.

This inspiration that keeps evolving. Therefore, even in my moments of most despair, I try to remind myself often that I may not be able to see it now, but it is planting the seeds of inspiration and transformation that I need for the future. So hang on.

After three near-death experiences due to health complications and thinking that I would never walk again, that perhaps I wouldn't make it, I transformed that pain into my leadership for developing advocacy for women's health issues as well as economic empowerment and truly using this moment to create something new for my life and for others. Check-out the project **www.wee-globallive.com** that resulted after my last near-death experience.

Vision - The vision is a flash of energy that sparks clarity to all that you have been building from your inspiration. It is when you truly begin to draw the map of your dreams to success. You understand this is your grounding space from where you are organizing your thoughts, projects, emotions, and ensuring everything is in alignment with your higher purpose. It is the foundation and the baseline of how you move forward to lead your life, your faith, business, family, campaigns, organizations or whatever project you're involved in. This is the map that takes you to the next stage until life lets you know it is time to shift again. After all, we are all humans in evolution and so are our visions and missions in life, that must ring true to who we are in that moment, in space, in time. Remember to stay inspired and use each of these stages to transform you to the best life you want to live. For details about transformation and empowerment visit **www.roxanadamas.soy**

SHAREEN RIVERA

Rising Above

I was five years old the first time I got drunk. I was starving. We were upstairs with the neighbor lady, and my sister and I were set on the couch in front of the TV while she and my mom were drinking in the kitchen. I left to go home and find something to eat since there was no food there either. I scoured our cabinets crying, opening the refrigerator to see nothing but two wine coolers. I took them and had the neighbor kid, Gilbert, open it for me. I chugged mine down and grabbed his drink and drank it too.

My stomach was in knots from my hunger, and I started feeling dizzy. I went to the courtyard to play with the other kids and got into a fight with the manager's daughter, and the manager ended up dragging me home by my hair. She opened the screen door and threw me inside our empty apartment. I threw up all over the front room floor and I was scared my Mom would find out, so I covered it with the clean clothes on the couch.

From the time I can remember, I was always in survival mode; surviving the turbulent storms of having an alcoholic, mentally-ill mother and an elusive father; surviving the family chaos and toxic behaviors that were our norm.

My Grandparents gained custody of my sister and me when I was ten-years-old, and although we were taken care of, we continued to endure extreme trauma and hardships. I still had a lot of responsibility placed on my shoulders and witnessed so many things that no child should ever have to witness.

Almost every week my Grandparents used to prepare me for their death. They'd constantly remind me that they are old and sick and if they die it is up to me to make sure my sister and I aren't separated and that I have to take care of my deaf Uncle who lived with us because he has nobody. They brainwashed me to believe that the rest of the family were jealous of the fact that they are raising us, so they won't take us in, therefore it is up to me.

I felt so much pressure and anxiety all the time wondering what I was going to do, dreading the day they die, and thinking about how I will survive if they did. I'd wake up in the middle of the night to go watch my Grandparent's breath to make sure they're alive.

I didn't know how to cope with it. I was always very controlling, emotional and anxious as a child. My Grandparents didn't take us to church but would take us to church conventions and it was there that I found my relationship with Christ, and for the first time in my life I felt the everlasting peace and happiness that comes when finding Jesus. I got baptized at 12-years old. I still attribute me giving my life to the Lord as the reason I was protected afterward through tribulations that should have broken me.

I was socially awkward when I started high school because of my seriousness. It was hard for me to relate to other kids my age or find things to talk about. I would see all the kids acting so carefree and wanted to be like that, so I became a follower, picking up horrible habits just to get people to like me. I started hanging out with the potheads, and at 13 years old I was smoking cigarettes and weed and skipping school.

I knew it was wrong, but it was the first time since finding Christ that I had another escape. My Grandparents were distracted caring for my sister at the time who was diagnosed with a severe form of Tourrette Syndrome, and my Mom was battling her addiction and mental illness while also still living with us. Consequently, I'd be left to fend for myself most of the time, with a lot of freedom.

I would be able to stay at my girlfriend's house for weeks at a time, doing things that no 13-year old should have the freedom to do. During my Sophomore summer, I found myself addicted to cigarettes, ecstasy, and weed. I was mean when I wasn't high, anxious, didn't care about anything and reckless. My Grandma found pills in my backpack and I grabbed my bag and ran out the door. I went with a few girlfriends and a guy friend to this park where one of my friends brought a gallon of Vodka they had stolen. I had never drank alcohol before, but I didn't care. I grabbed the vodka bottle and to prove how bad I was, I started taking gulps. I don't remember how many gulps I took, but it was enough to make my friend grab it from me.

Hours later the fire department was at my friend's house getting my naked body out of the shower and I was taken to the hospital to have my stomach pumped. I woke up with handcuffs chaining me to the hospital bed, my Grandma slapping my face, and nurses and doctors all around me. They kept me on hold in the psych ward, and every time I woke up there was someone sitting there taking notes, asking me if I was trying to commit suicide, if I had thoughts of dying, and probing me about everything.

The next day I was released to go home, and my Grandparents let me leave to go to my friend's house. I was planning on getting high, but God had another plan for me. I truly believe that people are brought into your life for a reason, and for me, I believe that God brought someone into my life that would guide me away from all these horrible things. I met my first boyfriend. I was 15 and he was 18. He was handsome, drove a Pontiac, with a good family and job. Right when we met, I instantly wanted to be a better person. We talked about Christ, liked the same music, had the same values and were inseparable. From that point on, I never did another drug again and got back to writing, reading and being healthy.

I started my Junior year with a fresh mindset, stopped hanging out with those kids, and started getting all A's. My boyfriend would pick me up during my lunch hour. For the first time, I felt wanted but to be wanted by a grown man, validated my worth.

We would go to concerts, parties, and trips on the weekends. He took me to Hawaii and vacations. I felt like an adult, and at only 16 years old we were talking about marriage. My Grandparents agreed to sign the paperwork for us to get married and insisted that, in fact, I do marry.

Thank God that his parents were sensible and swiftly intervened, but I thought that this was it. Of course, things change as you get older, and by the time I was 19, we had grown apart.

We slowly started spending our free time with friends, and I had gotten a fake ID when I was still in high school, so at 20 years old we'd go out to clubs separately with our friends. One weekend my girlfriend and I decided to go to a salsa club called, Miami's, in downtown San Jose, and it was that night I met my ex-husband, who was seven years older. We instantly hit it off, and it felt like being swept in a whirlwind. I was drawn to him and even told my girlfriend that I was going to marry him.

I broke up with my boyfriend to date my ex-husband who was seven years older than me, three children, with baby mama drama, and the whole works. Everyone told me I was crazy. I didn't care. No one understood what I was doing. I didn't even understand what I was doing. From the outside, I had it all going for me. I drove a black convertible mustang, 20 years old and super fit, had a good job for my age at a law firm, in college, and money saved. The problem was that I didn't see myself from that perspective. As a very naïve young adult, I was completely oblivious of how one decision can dramatically alter my life forever, and I lived in a constant reactive state. I still saw myself as the young girl with no food, being abused, and looking for someone to save her, who desperately wanted to belong somewhere and to feel like I mattered.

Our relationship started off immediately like a rollercoaster. I moved in with him three months after meeting, and we were breaking up, getting back together, arguing, and lots of inconsistent behavior, verbal and emotional abuse, but I already equated love with pain, so like I did with everyone else in my life, I kept trying to understand him.

Two years later I purchased my own condo during the holiday season and I found myself in this condo alone while he was out until all hours of the night doing God knows what, and when he was home, I was finding inappropriate text messages in his phone from other women. I was ready to finally leave. I had enough, and I was going to make the big leap right after the New Year to give him time to find a place to live.

Thanksgiving morning, we were at my sister's boyfriend's house and were woken up to his cell phone ringing non-stop. He rolled out of the bed and answered to his Mom asking if he was ok. He said, "What are you talking about Mom?" She started crying and said, "You don't know? Marylou died last night in a car accident." Marylou was the mother of his three children. At that very moment, it was as if time stood still and all we could feel was the heaviness of reality hitting us.

I did not know what my place was amidst the chaos. I couldn't find it in my heart to leave him after this tragedy, yet, he was with her family and his children mourning her loss. I wasn't welcome to be with them, his two oldest sons now hated me, his family blamed me cause they said if he wasn't with me he'd be with her, my Grandparents were trying to save their home but it was looking dim, the following week my Mom was found behind a dumpster in a parking lot almost dead and was in ICU, and that same week I found out I was pregnant. The walls of my life felt like they were crashing down, and I had nowhere to go and no one to turn to. I gathered the courage to tell my Grandma, and she told me to keep the baby, that it's God's will, and it doesn't matter if he's around to help me; that I could get on welfare and food stamps. That seemed like a complete nightmare to me.

I couldn't even imagine how I was going to do this alone. After being shunned by him and his entire family I decided that I'd move back in with my Grandparents to figure things out. I left him in my condo since he had nowhere to go.

Right after Christmas I told him I was pregnant, and he wanted me to keep it and then a few days later told me it's best I don't. For the first time in my life, I thought about killing myself. I felt so lost, alone, unwanted and scared. I slept at my girlfriend's house that week just so I wouldn't be alone because my thoughts scared me. I made an appointment at Planned Parenthood even though I didn't fully comprehend what I was doing. I knew abortions were against Christianity, but I really didn't understand why. I didn't think the baby had a heartbeat or was alive. I wasn't aware of how energy worked or the circle of life.

I was completely numb from all the trauma within the span of one month, and as the doctor played Beethoven while performing the procedure an overwhelming surge of sadness came through my body up through my throat and I started crying uncontrollably. The assistant got my friend who was waiting in the lobby and she came and held my hand and stroked my hair while the life was taken out of me. If ever there was a regret I had, it was the decision I made that day.

For the next two years, everything was a tumultuous rollercoaster. He proposed on Valentine's Day in front of my Grandparents who were, of course, elated, but four months later after the invitations were sent out, he canceled the wedding. I moved in and out multiple times. Both of our drinking and clubbing was out of hand. It wasn't as bad as before her death, but we were still out at least twice a week, hungover twice a week, and living the epitome of mediocrity. We couldn't save any money or get ahead on anything.

He left without telling me or the boys one evening while I was in the shower and went to a friend's house, turned his phone off, and came home belligerently drunk at 4am. I was devastated. I was yelling and crying, demanding answers. The kids heard everything from their room. I could hear the oldest boy soothing the cries of his brother. I left the house beat up. He had hit me before, but never this bad. My hair matted, bruises all over my arms and legs and lip busted. I sat in my car trying to think of where to go, but I felt too ashamed to show up at my Grandparents' like this. I couldn't let my sister or cousins see me this way, they all looked up to me, and because of this toxic relationship, I no longer had friends. So, I went to my gym at 5am, and sat in the steam room and cried out to God.

I mustered my strength to get dressed, and as I put on heavy makeup to cover up the bruises and bags under my eyes, I didn't recognize the young woman staring back at me anymore. Where was that strong, smart, ambitious woman that I thought I was?

That day I felt like I was nothing, and I decided enough was enough. I knew I had nowhere to go. My Grandparents were in the process of moving from the home I grew up in, because it was foreclosing, and I didn't want to add to their stress.

I decided to call my mom's ex-boyfriend who was fond of me. He was a 70-year old man, that had a nice house in the Los Gatos hills, and was always trying to offer me help. He agreed to let me stay there for a few months while I saved money to get my own place, and in one month I had enough saved for a studio. I was so proud the day I moved into my small studio all by myself. I didn't have much to move in, but it was all mine.

I decided to enroll back into college to finish my Associates, and I was trying to keep myself busy as much as possible, but he wouldn't stop trying to get me back. He'd follow me from work back to my studio and would show up every day on my porch at 5am to make sure no one was with me. I tried to date, but he'd blow up my phone and leave me love songs on my voicemail, sometimes waiting in front of my studio for me to come home. He begged and pleaded promising he'd never hurt me again. I told my Grandparents, and my Grandma reminded me that it was the woman who makes a relationship work.

I gave him an ultimatum, and the terms were either he never lays a hand and on me and marries me or leaves me alone. He agreed to get married and promised he'd never hit me again, and three days later we eloped in Reno with my family there, me wearing the dress I bought for our original planned wedding, without his children, and with no wedding rings. None of that mattered to me.

Six months later we were arguing in the car after having some drinks and he slapped me while driving to a co-worker's house to go on a double date. He got out and walked up the door as if nothing happened. I went inside feeling numb, playing the part, but inside I was screaming, wanting to tell my co-worker what had happened and cry. I got very good at playing the part. Even though the physical abuse stopped for some time, the constant verbal, mental and emotional abuse was a daily thing. I found myself tolerating behavior that I never thought possible. I was left alone with his children, cooking, cleaning, doing homework, while he was out at the bars, hanging with friends, and pretty much doing whatever he wanted.

Maya Angelou once said, "When someone shows you who they are, believe them the first time." I truly believe if I would have read that back then it would have changed my life. I kept thinking I could change him if I just loved him enough, and with time he'd see what he has and appreciate me.

Before I met him I used to write poems and share them with anyone who would listen. I used to avidly read and be excited to share what I learned. I would write in my journals but stopped sharing my poetry. I stopped thinking much about what I wrote.

With time, his happiness was all that mattered to me. I would do anything and did do everything to try to make him happy. His happiness came before my own. Yet, nothing I did seemed good enough. I'd cook lavish meals for him and my stepsons, and he'd always find one thing that he thought was wrong. I used to take it so personally, thinking I must be a horrible cook. I must be stupid to not do it right after all these years. Now, I realize that his issues went hand in hand with my issues and together we did this toxic dance. I was completely co-dependent on him validating me, on the outside world validating my relationship and thinking we had this picture-perfect little family, and between the two I received the validation I needed to feel worthy. Four years later, we decided that it was time to have a baby. I thought I was ready. I desperately wanted to feel connected to him, and to be a mother.

A few months later I found out I was pregnant, and the joy was soon traded for grief when my Grandpa suddenly was hospitalized, and we were told he had a few days to live. I screamed in the hospital hallway and fell to my knees sobbing. I used to fear this day as a child, and now it was here.

The next week was a nightmare. I wanted my husband to be with me. I needed him. I begged him to come to the hospital and stay with me since it was my turn to stay the night with Grandpy. He came five hours later, stumbling in the hallways, drunk, slurring his words. I was by my Grandpa's bedside holding his hand trying to sleep, and my husband was trying to make me have sex with him. I was crying, begging him to stop, and with each no, he was getting more and more aggressive. I could feel my unconscious Grandfather squeezing my hand as if he knew what was happening. The nurse finally came in because I was crying so loud, and he backed away and left me there. I had to take a taxi home in the morning and was so numb that I didn't even care if he was sorry or not. Two days later at 3am my Grandpa left this earth while holding me and my sister's hands, my cousins standing at the end of the bed, and my aunt singing The Old Rugged Cross.

I drove home distraught, and I truly felt like I didn't know if I could take care of myself right for the baby. I couldn't eat or sleep that day. All I wanted to do was cry. He left to go to work and that night he went out with his friends instead of staying home to be with me, and as I laid in the bed alone grieving over my Grandpa, I could feel God talking to me, telling me to leave and stay with my Grandma. I shook that feeling off because it's the woman that makes it work. I can't leave my husband, I thought to myself. I'm pregnant. *I now know that in the middle of a storm, God will speak to you. Those "gut feelings" that you shrug off cause it's easier to ignore them than listen, is really God trying to direct you out of the storm. The more you ignore, the deeper into the storm you go. The deeper I decided to go.*

As my pregnancy progressed, my doctors were worried about my weight gain and blood pressure. I was told I had preeclampsia. I had to go in every week for two-hour testing, and three days past my due date I started experiencing contractions.

They rushed me in for an emergency C-section because my son's heartbeat was dropping. At 2:02 pm I had my son. As they laid his naked body on my chest and attached him to my breast, I finally felt real love.

That moment everything that mattered in my life changed. I wanted to be a better woman for my son. The doctor wanted me to stay in the hospital because my blood pressure wasn't lowering, and three days later my husband was tired of sleeping on the couch and told me to tell them that I wanted to go home. So,

I did. I signed the papers against the doctor's will, and the nurse told me I was going to be released at 5pm. Soon after my husband told me he was going to Chilis to watch the Raider game. I was so worried because I knew once he starts drinking, he doesn't stop. I kept asking him to please stay, but he assured me he'd be back.

Five o'clock pm came and I was sitting in the room waiting, and the nurse rolled my wheelchair into the hallways holding my newborn son. I sat there for three hours, calling my husband, crying and begging him to come get us. I finally had to put my pride away and call my sister to pick us up. I left the hospital with no car seat, holding my newborn baby in the backseat, promising him that it's going to be ok.

The next day I couldn't go pee, and the following day I was so bloated my foot couldn't fit into my sandal. The nurse said to come in immediately, so my sister took me back to the hospital. They admitted me right away because my blood pressure was through the roof and they said I could have a stroke or heart attack at any time, and my kidneys were shutting down.

They put me on some drip, and I was bedridden for the next three days. I could hear babies crying in the hallways, and could feel my breasts filling up with milk, and the nurses would come and pump them. I felt so depressed. My sister would come to see me as much as she could, but I was all alone most of the time, and in-between consciousness I admitted to them that I wanted to die. The nurses called my husband and told him to come to the hospital and bring the baby.

After three days of being on this drip, not eating or drinking anything, not walking, and barely being awake, the doctor told me that everything was finally stabilized. I had lost 27 pounds of fluid, and was told that if I could get up and walk to the chair across the room that I could most likely go home the next day.

All I wanted to do was see my baby, and I focused on that while I lifted myself up. I looked down at my body and didn't recognize myself. My stomach was loose and big, and my legs looked like jello. I started to cry and looked up at the nurse, and she assured me that it's ok to be in shock. That it's normal because my body looked different when I came into the hospital. I looked away and told myself that I'll get back into shape, it doesn't matter right now. I just need to get home to be with my son, and I forced myself up, and all I could do was stand in place. My legs felt so heavy and cemented to the ground and ached. My C-section scar was throbbing, and my entire body was extremely weak. I couldn't move my legs, and fell back onto the bed.

The nurse came to help me, and I pushed her away and told her I could do it. I pushed myself up again and started yelling at myself to move, and I don't know how, but I started walking to the chair and with each step, I was crying and yelling at myself to keep going. By the time I got to the chair, there were three nurses behind me clapping and one was crying. They came up to me and hugged me, and we started crying together. *I learned that day that when all else fails you, your soul will stand up inside you and give you the strength you need. Never give up on yourself.*

I went home the next day and the journey of motherhood completely changed me. I wanted to be better. I wanted better things, and dedicated myself to being healthy, getting my relationship back with God, and trying to enforce good healthy habits into my family. Things got better and my husband's business started growing and we were doing well financially. For the next two years, we finally seemed to be getting a groove together as parents. I loved and appreciated my husband and felt God's blessings in my life.

One day I left work early to go to my regular OB-GYN annual check-up. The doctor asked me the routine question, when did I last have my period. I told her that I was set to get it that day, but I hadn't yet. She insisted that I take a pregnancy test to be sure. I thought she was being ridiculous, because I wasn't exactly late, and I wanted to hurry and get home. I took the test to appease her. I waited in the room what seemed like a half-hour and out of frustration I gathered my things to leave. Right, when I was walking out of the door the doctor chased me down the hall and told me to come back to the room. "Shareen, my dear, you are very much pregnant."

I looked at her with a blank expression on my face, completely numb, and everything she said was a blur. I was on the pill. I took that pill faithfully every night and was baffled how this happened. She told me that there still is always a slight chance when on the pill.

All I could think about was, "How am I going to do this, and what if I get sick again?" I went home worrying about how I was going to tell him, and when I walked through the door he was sitting on the couch with this worried look on his face and I asked him what was going on, but he assured me nothing was wrong. I just blurted out that I was pregnant. He had a look of panic but was trying to seem happy. It was the same look on his face when we were driving to the courthouse to get our marriage certificate. *There are signs all around us, telling us the truth about our life, situation, and people. It is our job to pay attention to these signs and ask God for direction, and then when he gives us direction, to listen and follow. I did not understand any of this, and decided, once again, to ignore*

*the signs and PRETEND like everything was going to be fine. Living
in denial was safer than accepting the truth, but I learned it's also
more dangerous in the end.*

The next eight months went smoother than my first pregnancy.
We got a bigger house, and he was working a lot, but drinking
more too. I could tell he felt stressed, and I knew that his coping
mechanisms were to run away and hide so I was preparing myself during my pregnancy for that to happen. When neglect and
emotional abuse are your norm, you stop talking about it to other
people because it's normal. You find ways to deal and justify it,
and the way that I did this was to hold onto understanding why
he is the way he is. I understood him so well, so I justified his
behavior by understanding him and his past.

I took on the role of the peacemaker in the home, making sure that
none of the kids felt the stress or anger from him; making sure
everything went smooth and that there was very little for him to
do at home. I took on so much responsibility and was pouring into
everyone's cup but my own, that by the time I had my daughter, I
was completely depleted.

I was having contractions, and begged him, once again, to leave
his friend's house and come take me to the hospital. I fell asleep
waiting for him and decided to wait until the morning. The morning came and he left to go to a job. I was about to call a taxicab to
go to the hospital, but thankfully he finally came. It was like déjà
vu all over again. They told me that my blood pressure was raising
and scheduled an emergency c-section. I was having major anxiety because of what happened to me after I had my son. I could see
panic written all over his face as the doctor kept talking, and he
left to go to a "job" and came back afterward smelling like alcohol.

I went in for my c-section with major anxiety and came out with a baby and more anxiety. I begged the doctor to keep me for the full five days. I was dreading going home to do it all by myself with two babies. I spent those five days alone with my daughter, resting, wishing I could just stay in that room forever.

The day that I was released, my Grandma, Uncle, Son, and Husband were with me, and I could tell he was clearly just as overwhelmed as I was, throwing my bags in the car, cussing because I asked him to buckle the car seat in. I could barely get in our SUV, and he slammed my door. My Grandma saw the whole scene and was visibly upset too because she had no idea what took place behind closed doors.

The following morning, I called her in a panic. I never had called her telling her anything before. I was always scared to stress her out, but I felt hopeless. He had a fit of rage for something and threw a chair at our glass closet doors, breaking them, and left. I couldn't bend down to pick the glass up cause of my c-section, the babies were crying, and I could barely walk.

My Grandma came to my rescue and cleaned it all up and sat next to me, reminding me that it is the woman that makes it work and to give him his space. God will give me the strength, but it isn't right the way he is treating me and said she was going to talk to him.

Of course, her talk went to deaf ears. Over the next six months, our marriage regressed to the earlier days of us dating. I was left with two babies and stepsons while recovering from my c-section. Thank God my stepsons helped me as much as they could. I couldn't take my pain meds, because they made me sleepy and I had no one to watch my son during the day, so I'd take half of the dosage and force myself to walk outside while my son played. I forced myself to recover and not have to rely on anyone, especially him, for anything. His drinking got heavier and happy hour nights were more often, but I stopped caring as much because I started appreciating my own strength and seeing my own power.

My soul was standing up inside me again. I lost 60 pounds within the course of 3 months. When he got mad about me constantly going to the gym, I then converted our garage to a gym. When he got mad about me waking up early to work out cause of the kids, I then worked out at night. When the nighttime workouts were an inconvenience I then did it mid-day while the kids napped. I wasn't going to let him take this away from me. *It was through my workouts that I was gaining the mental strength, callousing my mind to stop worrying about him and pour into my own cup.*

That October, I received the mind shift I needed to wake the hell up. He came home hungover after leaving me and the kids for a weekend, not answering his phone. I was holding our 6-month old daughter yelling and crying, our son was standing at the bedroom doorway watching. I pushed him as he was walking away cussing at me to shut up. He turned around and kicked me in my chest. I fell to the ground, dropping our daughter, and turned and saw our son screaming and crying. I looked up at him as he carelessly walked away, and it was then that I heard my soul tell me "NO MORE! ENOUGH IS ENOUGH SHAREEN!"

I left my kids with my stepsons and got in my car and drove. I parked by my Grandparent's old house that I grew up in and cried and screamed out to God once again.

I begged God to help me. Tell me what to do. Give me the strength. Give me the power to show my children different. Give me the support I needed to leave and let me have a better life for my children.

Let me tell you what happens when you cry out to God in the moment of hopelessness and vulnerability- he listens. You may feel lost, but it is then that you are being found and carried. God listened, and I found strength in myself that I never knew. I came home as a different woman. I walked to the end of the bed and let him know that I am no longer in love with him and things are going to change. He called me names and told me to shut up and brushed me off as he laid there watching TV, never making eye contact, but the next three months was definitely hell for him and everyone in the house, including me.

When you let someone walk all over you for years, and then suddenly you have boundaries and demand respect, it becomes a problem. I no longer was tolerating verbal abuse, physical abuse, emotional abuse and I was standing up for myself. When he went out with his friends, I'd let him and not bother him, but then I'd leave the next night and go out myself. I never used to go out alone before, but I started giving him a taste of his own medicine.

I stopped sleeping with him. I stopped cooking and serving him, and if the laundry needed to be done and I didn't have time, then oh well. I stopped spending my nights crying and spent them visualizing my new life and getting excited. I was busy selling everything I could get my hands on through eBay and Craigslist. After work, I'd pick up free items on Craigslist and resell it. I talked my boss into doubling my bonus for Christmas and to give it to me early, and I was saving every dollar in a jacket in my closet. It just so happened that my best friend at the time wanted to move to San Jose, so I let her move in with us without his blessing, because I knew that we could be roommates when the time came.

I slowly became numb to anything my husband was feeling and consequences for anything that I was doing, because I wanted out. I gave him the choice to leave or I leave. I told him he could leave my stepsons, and I'd take care of them, so he started searching for a place. During that process, I made the huge mistake of having an affair with a man I met while out one night. I threw ten years of loyalty out of the door and opened a whole new door into my life called guilt.

This was a way for the devil to somehow take hold in my life to stop or slow my blessing, and that is what happens before you're going to be blessed-you are attacked to distract you, to make you lose your focus, to hinder your blessing, to stop you being purposeful. I heard TD Jacks say one day, "That a robber doesn't rob an empty house. If you're under attack, it's because your house has something." There was much to steal in my house, and I didn't even know it, so I left my door unlocked and wasn't aware of how everything is connected and sent, either by God or the devil.

This was my second battle with true guilt, and I've learned that guilt eats you from the inside out. This affair not only caused guilt, but after my husband found out, he then blamed this affair for the reason for me leaving, and it relieved him of the burden of taking responsibility for anything. I was forced to move out in one week because it was so bad at our house and was no longer safe for me. My clothes were thrown out of the closet twice. I had things thrown at me across the room. He shattered my phone and refused to replace it. I wasn't allowed to be in a room alone. I woke up to being interrogated, followed around the house, yelled and cussed at every second.

The day that I left I felt so empowered like I could take on the world. I got my own apartment, rented a moving truck, and got a few of my cousin's friends to help me, and I left him laying on the bedroom floor wondering how this even happened. I thought that everything was going to get better from here on out, but this was just the start of my new beginning.

After I left, I had no one else to blame or point the finger at as to why I wasn't happy. I could only blame the woman looking back at me in the mirror; this foreign woman that I didn't recognize or even know. I had no idea who the woman I was alone with. I had no idea what to do with myself when he had the kids and I'd come home at night to no one needing me, no one to cook for, no one to distract myself from dealing with my issues.

I finally was left alone with just me, myself and the big elephant in the room that was my insecurities and undealt with trauma. It was through my isolation that I started the journey of healing.

Healing is a lifelong journey of shedding the layers of yourself, of your truth, of your reality, and awakening to your being. I realized the longer I held on to the truths that I was taught as a child, doing the same things, then I was always going to remain the same woman. I had to release these truths like, "The woman is the one that makes it work", and all of the old habits that I had gained through the course of it all, like tv watching, drinking during depression, and living in a reactive state, and just be still.

It's been a long process of discovering myself, but I now know that *progression is irreversible*. Once you get on the self-development spectrum there is no turning back, so even if you fall off and revert to your old ways, you're aware of it and just get right back on. I didn't have anyone to advise me or mentor me, but I found mentors in people that I knew were living the truth and successful. I started scanning YouTube for motivation or healing, and I learned meditation through Dr. Deepok Chopra. I learned the power of stillness through Wayne Dyer. I resonated with Oprah and Maya Angelou's stories of resiliency and wisdom. I learned how to live on purpose through Tony Robbins. TD Jakes taught me the power of forgiveness, and the need to stay woke to spiritual attacks. I learned to stay a student of life and to remain open.

In the stillness of my being, I started becoming awakened to who I was, and my eyes were finally opened. I now see life through a different lens. I now know I am in control of me, of my feelings, of what I can do in life- we all are, and that is empowering. I wanted to share that with every woman that has gone through any kind of adversity, who has lost themselves through the pain and sadness and stopped dreaming. I made the decision to publish my first book telling my story, and it has been a continual upward spiral, because, as I said, progression is irreversible. I've dedicated my life to turning all this pain into a purpose by helping others believe in themselves, by breaking these generational curses, and by trying every single day to be the best version of myself possible. Some days I do fall, but I promise, I always get myself back up because I will always rise above. I promise you that if I can, you can too.

To learn more about my Ghostwriting business, books, tv show, or to book me to speak, please visit **www.shareenrivera.com**, or email at: **contactme@shareenrivera.com**

VIRGINIA MADUENO

Hope And Faith
Through Despair

I am in the midst of an overpowering and destructive hurricane in my life right now. Sometimes I have to sit back and remember exactly who I am, and what has led me to where I am today. For too long, I have been wearing a mask that has helped me to overcome the most difficult of circumstances but has left me with the uncompromising question of

"Who really am I" I am the middle daughter of Rojelio and Juana Arauza, immigrants from Penjamillio Michoacán Mexico. My parents immigrated to the U.S. with three children in 1965. I was their first American born daughter. My mother used to joke and say I crossed the border illegally since she was pregnant with me when she immigrated to the U.S. Life was especially hard for my parents back then, much as it was for many immigrants coming to the U.S., not knowing the language. Mom often tells the story of when I was just shy of my first birthday, I had gotten very sick. She said she took me to the doctor, but my condition did not improve. It got worse within a week. When mom saw me getting stiff joints, she knew something serious was going on, it was not the flu as the doctor had said.

She again took me back to that doctor, but he could not tend to me as he had too many patients that day according to mom, so his office staff recommended another doctor in a neighboring medical complex. Mom desperate to get me medical attention did not care who would take me. She just wanted me seen and treated.

I am a true believer in faith and things happening for a reason. My mother remembers that moment when the new physician took one look at me in his office, and he immediately diagnosed me. I had bacterial meningitis. Mom was told I needed to be hospitalized immediately.

There was no going back. My condition was grave. Mom remembers walking home with her very sick baby to have my father drive us to the hospital. My father was the only one working and his pay as a field laborer was not much back then.

Upon arrival at Scenic General Hospital, the first thing my parents were asked for was health insurance or payment for services. Unfortunately, this was not acceptable by the hospital staff and consequently, I was denied the health care I desperately needed. Mom says she felt her heart sink. She knew they would take me home and I would undoubtedly die there. As my parents left the hospital, the doctor who properly diagnosed me was pulling into the hospital and met them at the bottom of the entrance stairs.

He asked them where they were taking me, and he explained to them that I needed to be hospitalized or I would die without proper medical treatment. My parents explained to the doctor that

I was denied medical care due to a lack of health insurance and my father's meager earnings. Mom said that the doctor grabbed me from her arms, marched up the stairs into the admitting office and the yelling started. She doesn't know what was said because it was all in English. My mom was not able to hold me for nearly a month after I was admitted, she would only be able to see me through a small window on the door of my room since I was now in isolation. My life was saved, and I can only thank that doctor who saved my life. He was my advocate. Mom said we never received a medical bill for my treatment.

To this day it is a mystery of how this was resolved without any notice or billing statement to my parents. There is no question; God wanted me to stay on this earth for a reason and I suppose that is the reason why I have chosen to use my voice to be an advocate and leader in my community.

One of my earliest memories growing up includes pulling into our newly rented home in the outskirts of Escalon, California, where I still recall the address 20228 Harold Avenue. The house was adjacent to my Tio and Tia Jesus and their family.

Although there were many good memories such as me riding my bike in the country, running through my uncle's cornfields and orchards, swinging on a tree swing or playing poker with my Papa Che, this would also be the home where I would find trauma and painful experiences that still haunt me to this day.

My father was a heavy drinker, an alcoholic, and his drinking combined with his short temper and Mexican machismo was a very bad combination. I have two very haunting and vivid memories from our Escalon home, the night we were left outside, me sitting on my mom's lap with my brother and sisters close by. We were locked out of our home not because we didn't have keys but because dad came home drunk and threw us out. It was cold and I can remember my mother crying.

I am not sure if he beat her that night, but clearly, there was a fight. Her cries that night would not be as intense as the night where my father beat mom so badly that my mother would need medical attention. I remember the chaos as I walked into my parent's bedroom where I saw the blood on my mother's face, her intense crying and my aunt and cousins at her side. I was scared and confused to see my mother in that condition, but I was too young to understand that the responsible party was my father. I suppose this is why I have such deep compassion for victims of domestic violence and have chosen to advocate on behalf of this cause for years.

Escalon was my home from the time I was three or four years old until I finished the 1st grade at Dent Elementary. At age seven my family moved to Riverbank into new government housing. My parents were part of a federal housing program called "Self Help Housing", where they were required to invest in their own time and sweat equity in building our new home. It was small but it was new. I still remember the avocado green paint inside our home, which was quite popular in the '70s. My parents were field workers and then eventually found seasonable employment at Tri-Valley Growers, a local canning company.

During their time working at Tri-Valley Growers, I learned about organized labor through my parent's involvement with Teamsters and remember joining them when they participated in their first strike where I attended a rally with them at John Thurman Field a local baseball stadium. My parents migrated for work specifi-cally during the cherry season as well as to various other parts of the valley for apricots, peaches, blackberries, and tomatoes. They sometimes traveled as far as Oregon and Washington to pick cherries I often traveled with them and remember those hot summer days driving in my dad's Ford pick-up truck with no AC but rather with rolled down windows letting the hot air attempt to cool us down.

I was very timid growing up. I suppose having three older siblings made it difficult to have a voice. I was also the youngest in the family for seven years until my sister Anjelica was born. It was a challenging time for me.

No one paid attention to me anymore. I wasn't the youngest and clearly, someone else had mom and dad's attention. This was not a good place for me, so I learned to be visible by becoming a translator and advocate for my mom and dad. I often interpreted for them since they did not speak English. I would often read and write letters for my mom to her sisters in Mexico since mom could not read or write, she did not have the opportunity to go to school.

I now reflect and realize I was a bit of a tomboy growing up. I was by all accounts supposed to be a boy after all my parents already had two girls and one boy before I was born so I would naturally be the next boy. I remember wearing baseball caps, climbing trees and loved to be outdoors, rode my bike as much as I could and loved to clown around.

I also smoked at a very young age. My grandfather (Papache) would allow us to smoke with him while we played poker, to this day I still enjoy the smell of someone lighting a cigarette.

I helped my parents as much as I could by working in the fields with them. I recall waking up at as early as 4 am; mom was always in the kitchen getting our lunch ready at that early hour. Mom and Dad would crack two eggs in a glass of wine to get their morning started. Not sure what that was about, but it seemed to work for them, and I suppose gave them the nutrients for the early morning start.

When I was old enough, I stopped working in the fields with my parents and I took a part-time job as an office helper through Migrant Education while I was attending high school. I was a good student and did well enough to earn various notable awards and recognitions as well as scholarships to go to college after high school. I loved helping others and always saw myself filling in roles where I could serve.

We lived modestly in our Riverbank home and my parents who were very strict with me and my siblings did not allow us to get involved or active outside the home, we didn't have many friends come over either. My parents were private people and did not want anyone to know our business. This practice made me do the same where I always kept our family affairs private. I often defied my parents by getting involved in student government or the school site council and got active in high school clubs working on fund-raisers to raise money for Sacramento for a week.

This was a pivotal event in my life. It was the beginning of what I consider my political awakening. I was introduced to leaders and activists at this conference including actor Edward James Olmos who starred in the film "The Ballad of Gregorio Cortez" to highlight the issues of social injustice on Mexicans. It was also the time where I was introduced to California Senator Art Torres and saw for the first time an elected official who looked like me and I thought one day could be me. I was a bit nerdy, not very social but always tried to have a sense of humor. I always had a special place for service in my community, from helping to serve Thanksgiving dinners to local seniors, urging the Riverbank City Council to proclaim Riverbank as a culturally diverse city in lieu of the KKK's blatant presence or raising money for student schol-arships while I was a high school student. I was also active in college with MEChA, CIL (Chicanos in Law), CRLA, and learned more about politics and worked on the reelection campaign for Richard Patterson to the Modesto City Council and of course remember the day I traveled to Stockton CA to attend a press conference where Dianne Feinstein announced her candidacy for US Senate.

I was starting to get hooked into the world of politics. During col-lege, I met my husband Ramiro. We dated for a few years (seven to be exact) and after I graduated from college and found my career path in communications, I got married and we made our home in my hometown of Riverbank.

We built our home and raised our three boys there while I worked for Stanislaus County as a marketing manager and public information officer prior to starting my own PR and marketing firm which I still own today. Owning my own company has been challenging but also rewarding and has allowed me the opportunity to get reengaged and involved in my community while championing social justice causes that I consider important. Owning my own firm also allowed me to get national exposure and acceptance and I am still humbled by the two national distinctions I earned, Trailblazer Business of the Year by the National Association of Women Business Owners and Wells Fargo and the Anna Maria Arias Memorial Business of the Year by Latina Style Magazine. These two particular events were very uplifting and fulfilling moments in my career but also affirmed that all is possible even for the daughter of immigrant farmworkers.

STRIVING FOR REPRESENTATIVE LEADERSHIP

When my youngest children, twin boys turned five, I enrolled them in kindergarten, I told my husband my goal was to get active again in the community after taking a few years off to raise my young family. Ironically the week I signed up my twins for school I read in the local paper that the Riverbank City Council had a vacancy. That was a clear sign for me; I would apply for that appointment. I didn't have any experience in governance but I figured my role, as a mother and small business owner would be a good fit for the city council to help advocate for a safe and healthy community for our families as well as to help more small business owner's open doors in our city.

The population of Riverbank is very diverse, over 55% are Latino and we did not have a single person on the City Council to reflect that diversity. I considered myself a good communicator and storyteller and after a round of interviews with 12 other candidates on our local cable television station, I was victorious and was appointed to the City Council. I served on the Riverbank City Council from 2005 to 2008 and ran for Mayor in 2008, where I lost but then ran again in a special election in 2009 and won by less than 150 votes over my main opponent.

I didn't know much about campaigning or running an election the first time I ran for Mayor. I didn't know about high propensity voters or dedicated lists of registered voters. All I knew about was publicity, marketing, and promotions, which helped me get my name out the first time, but it was clearly not enough to get me elected.

Thankfully I met some amazing and wonderful women after my defeat, such as former State Senator Deborah Ortiz and Raquel Pimentel. These two ladies promised to help me and did they ever. Never had I seen such profound knowledge or dedication to a campaign operation. Raquel would even spend the night at my house when the nights were too long for her to drive home.

I was a novice but quickly started to learn that campaigns are much like a business, the more you put into a campaign the more you get out and learned that politics is not for the faint at heart. It is considered a contact sport and you are subjected to the vilest and scrupulous of people's behaviors. This would also be the time where I would start to see the racial divide and blatant racism come out in my hometown that has ultimately affected my family in unimaginable ways.

I've subjected my family through so much by being politically involved. My 14-year old son was viciously assaulted soon after I was elected mayor where he suffered severe head trauma. Law enforcement suspected the attack was politically motivated but was never proven. Almost 10 years later, my son and family are still experiencing retaliation for my political involvement because I'm not only a woman but a Latina woman who often speaks truth to power.

One of my opponents whose last name was White had the audacity of printing his large campaign signs to read WHITE MAYOR, not White for Mayor but WHITE MAYOR for Riverbank. This would be a clear indication of what I would face during my time as mayor. Never in my life had I felt such a sense of elation and validity when I was elected Mayor of Riverbank. It felt as though this win was not mine alone but a win for my community, my "gente", the people, who up to this point had been forgotten and had no voice. I was elected the first Latina Mayor and first Latina elected official for my hometown of nearly 23,000 residents in 2009.

There were family, friends, supporters and some who came were just curious to see the first Latina sworn into office. My mother came to my house before the ceremony started; she came and gave me a blessing. I almost felt as though I was getting married again and leaving my home again. This would be a tremendous responsibility and one that came with a lot of sacrifices, heartache as well as with some very positive outcomes as well. It is not easy to be the first in something. Sometimes you have to make up the rules as you go along while trying to make sure you don't screw things up. On one hand, I had many people rooting for me and asking for my help, especially the Spanish speaking community.

They felt comfortable enough to be able to call on me, someone who they could relate to. I loved meeting people and loved to see how the city could become a model for other cities, and most importantly, I wanted to be a mayor for all. I never saw my position of mayor as someone on a pedestal; on the contrary, I saw the position as one who would be embedded with the people. It was wonderful to be a part of the community leadership and to see the community embrace its new leader.

However, not everyone was happy with my election and there were those who refused to accept that the leader of their city was a woman and worst yet a brown woman. I managed to stay focused and positive in spite of all the controversies that came with managing the city but during this time I also saw the devastating toll that my role in politics played in my own personal life, my family and my children. I was naïve on politics and how dirty politics can be and how the line is not drawn with you as the politician but how it goes much further to impact those you most love.

I loved meeting people and loved to see how the city could become a model for other cities, and most importantly, I wanted to be a mayor for all. I never saw my position of mayor as someone on a pedestal; on the contrary, I saw the position as one who would be embedded with the people. It was wonderful to be a part of the community leadership and to see the community embrace its new leader.

Our communities, our state, and our country are evolving and with this evolution comes a time to recognize that our leadershipneeds to evolve as well. We cannot sit idle and let others make decisions for us but rather we need to be active and engaged if we want to see a true change that reflects the needs of our community.

I believed that immigrants should be thankful to live in this great country and not ask for more or worst yet question our authority. How could I think like this? In great part, I think it had to do with how I was raised. My parents had little to no education, they were and are modest people who worked hard and were grateful to live in a country that gave them an opportunity to build a home and raise a family.

Our country is in desperate need of leaders who represent all and who will be servants of the people and by the people and who can govern with an open heart and mind. Too many politicians want to run for office and stay in office because of their own individual agenda and self-propaganda. *Genuine leadership is when you give of yourself for the betterment of others.*

My mother who is probably the strongest woman I know showed me the value of standing up for oneself, she took her last round of abuse from my father and divorced him after 43 years. I continue to defy my role in my family and society by continuing to advocate on issues that I feel are important and are linked to social justice. We live in a time where more women are becoming leaders in our nation, state, and our communities. I chose to run for Congress in 2018, the year women were being challenged and asked to step up in lieu of our new president and his blatant attacks on women, immigrants and health care. I felt the need to step up. I questioned my ability to run for such a high office; did I have the stamina to take on such a critical role? Was my family willing to take this fight? Could I raise the money to get my name out there? I asked all the professional questions, but I didn't ask the personal questions; how would this affect me, my business, my marriage and most importantly my family?

These were the questions I should have asked a little more intensely.

Looking back to that time, I see that I was hiding from my reality and putting the needs of the community first before my own family.

For most of my life, I have been a mother, wife, community leader, advocate, entrepreneur, and activist. On my crusade for empow-erment, self-fulfillment and being a community advocate, I often wore a mask...a mask that helped to hide my insecurities, depres-sion, fears, and my troubles.

That mask prevented me and kept me from acknowledging my true self. While the world around me saw a confident and inde-pendent person, I gave into that perception that prevented me from being my genuine self and from showing my true vulnera-bilities... I no longer want to wear that mask, but rather I want to share with others, especially women the importance of emotional intelligence and being true to oneself. We deserve to feel every emotion and share those emotions as a testament to our identity and resilience. We need to accept ourselves for who we are and not for what people want us to be. I have learned to accept that my past is in the past, but my future is what I choose to do today and move forward.

As I work through my most difficult of personal situations today, I remind myself I am strong and resilient and lean on faith and hope to get me through my dark moments. I now know that I have the power to change my tomorrow by what I do and think today. "TRUTH IS STRONGER THAN FICTION."

I am a wife, mother, entrepreneur, small business owner and advocate but more importantly, I am Virginia Madueno, the daughter of immigrants who chose to be a voice so that others who didn't have one could be heard.

MISSION STATEMENT

VIVA is a movement where our purpose is to encourage women to live their life with Vision-Inspiration-Voice-Acceptance. We do this by creating a space for them where we can offer emotional support and connect them to the correct resources. Our committee includes strong women with certifications in suicide prevention, rescue from human sex trafficking, life coaches, health coaches and survivors of abuse.

Through the events we hold. women find a safe place where they can feel like they belong. We have young women in their teens to women in their 60's, all backgrounds, any ethnicity and all walks of life... still we join each other's journeys. No judgement, only encouragement in our community of sisterhood because no woman should ever feel alone or be left behind.

Mia Perez ~Founder of VIVA WOMEN

FOLLOW US:

FACEBOOK
https://www.facebook.com/vivawomenmp/

INSTAGRAM
https://www.instagram.com/vivawomen_/

WEBSITE
www.vivawomen.org

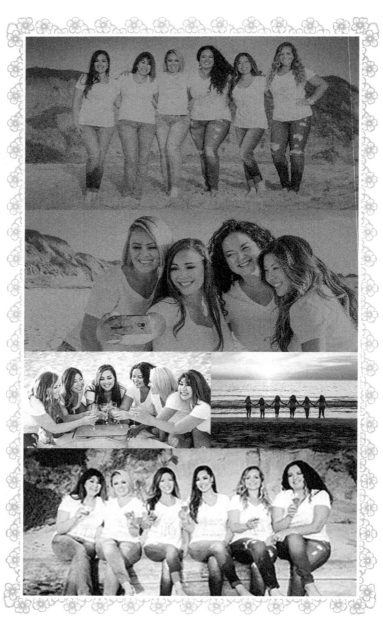